FAIRWAYS

9/2003

Dear Ben,

Happy 50th and many happy days on the Course!

The Adamsons

FAIRWAYS

INSPIRATION FOR THE
GOLF ENTHUSIAST

KEN ABRAHAM

PROMISE
PRESS
An Imprint of Barbour Publishing

Published by Promise Press, P.O. Box 719, Uhrichsville, OH 44683
http://www.barbourbooks.com

Member of the
Evangelical Christian
Publishers Association

Printed in the United States of America.

DEDICATION

To Paul, Toni, Sarah Jean, and Josie Azinger.
Thank you for the inspiration you have been to me,
both on and off the golf course.
You will always be the best in my book!

CONTENTS

Some Days Are Like That. 11

When You Really Need to Know 14

Playing Dirty 18

Family First 21

Christians at the Masters. 24

Don't Worry, Be Happy 29

Rolling 'Em Straight. 32

You Gotta Play by the Rules. 36

A Tee Time You Don't Want to Miss. 40

Baseball Power or Club-head Speed 45

What Comes Naturally 50

Now That's a Lousy Shot! 55

Your Good—God's Glory. 60

Mr. Pressure 65

Real Confidence. 70

Murder on the Green 73

How Much Mud? 76

Home on the Range 82

Money Matters. 86

When Words Can't Say Enough 90

Conquering Handicaps 94

A New Beginning. 98
The Real Thing. 101
Keep Your Eye on the Ball 106
Beauty and the Best 111
Avoiding Callouses. 114
A Matter of Taste 120
Giving God a Tip 126
Death, Where Is Your Sting?. 130
The Green You Don't Want to Hit. 135
Free Play 140
Honesty in All Things. 144
Honor to Whom Honor Is Due 150
How Much Is Enough?. 153
A Real Winner 158
Slow Play. 161
The Course Always Wins 164
Play to Win, but if You Don't 168
Straight Ahead 171
A Time to Speak. 174
Water Balls. 178
Confidence in the Face of Conflict 182
One Size Doesn't Fit All. 188
Playing on Empty. 191
Enjoying the Nineteenth Hole. 196

Idol Worship. 201
Integrity Counts 203
You're Not Alone 205
Our Thoughts Make a Difference 209
It's a Mental Game. 211
You Deserve a Break 214
Keep a Light Grip. 217
Perfect Is a Long Shot 220
When You Don't Get What You Want 224
Keep at It 226
The Pros and Cons of Anger. 228
Keep up the Energy 230
Little Big Man 233
Runner-up. 236
Seesaw Days. 238
Some Gimmes Aren't So Good. 240
The Great Equalizer 242
The Dues Have Been Paid 245

Notes 249

SOME DAYS ARE LIKE THAT

*I can do all things through Him
who strengthens me.*
PHILIPPIANS 4:13

Have you ever had a day when you wondered why you bothered to get out of bed, much less to go out on a golf course? Nothing seems to be going your way. Your golf swing feels out of sync, your putts are stopping millimeters away from the cup, and your shots off the tee are like misguided missiles. You feel like a failure, like you might as well hang it up and quit.

Former Vice President Spiro Agnew must have felt that way when he was playing in the 1971 Pro-Am at the Bob Hope Desert Classic in Palm Springs, California. The vice president meticulously went through his pre-shot routine, took his practice swing, stepped up to the ball, and promptly hit his drive into the gallery—not once, but twice—hitting three spectators with his first two tee shots.

Agnew packed up his clubs and withdrew from the tournament.

It's easy to quit when things are not going our way. Quitting takes little effort or fortitude. Some people quit before they get started; they feel they will not succeed so why bother to try?

God can change our thinking and attitudes if we will just give Him a chance. When our hearts are right with Him, and our desire is to bring honor to His name, He will show us how we can achieve our goals or accomplish that task that seems impossible.

Sure we may have some setbacks, disappointments, and failures. Everybody does from time to time. But remember, God is rooting for us and is ready and willing to help us. Sometimes, we sit back and wait for the Lord to perform a miracle (which He often does in spite of us), but we are too timid to get involved. But the apostle Paul declared with confidence, "I can do all things through Him who strengthens me" (Philippians 4:13). He wasn't being egotistical or cocky. Paul knew his strength and ability came from the Lord and that God expected him to step out in faith and attempt that which would be impossible apart from the supernatural power of Christ in him.

Don't be afraid to attempt great things for God. Read His Word and see what He wants you to do, what He wants you to be. Then step up to the ball and swing with confidence. God is with you, and He will strengthen you. He will help you.

PRAYER
Lord, help me to be patient with myself
when I make a mistake.
Let me dare to risk failure and
attempt something great for Your honor.

FURTHER READING
Philippians 4:4–19

WHEN YOU REALLY
NEED TO KNOW

Thy word is a lamp to my feet,
and a light to my path.
PSALM 119:105

Imagine for a moment that your drive lands deep in the rough. When at last you find your ball, you take a few practice swings, trying to gauge just how much oomph you will need to get out of this mess. You look for the pin, trying to figure out a yardage marker that might help you get a better idea of how far away your next shot should be. You are confused, uncertain, and—okay, let's admit it—just a bit frustrated that you hit your drive into such an uninviting location in the first place.

But never fear! The On Course Instructor is here. You reach into your pocket, pull out your On Course Instructor—a handheld computer—punch in the relevant data concerning your predicament, and presto! The On Course Instructor provides you with an instant golf lesson from a bona fide professional instructor concerning the precise (well, almost precise) circumstances in which you find yourself, and—best of all—how to successfully play out of that situation.

This is no joke. Thanks to a computer microchip, you can now carry a teaching pro with you at all times. The On Course Instructor comes with 4K of memory and is preprogrammed to help you in more than 130 shot situations.

How do you get out of the rough? Your On Course Instructor advises, "Use a three-quarter upright swing. Ball in center of stance. Hit down and through the ball. High finish-face target. Hands lead during impact. Strike behind the ball."

No word on whether the On Course Instructor can help you retrieve a ball from the pond.

Aren't you glad that God has provided a much more reliable "On Course Instructor" for His people? It's called the Bible. God has promised to guide and direct our paths, and although He may occasionally send a message by an angel or speak out of a burning bush, He more frequently speaks to us through His Word, the Bible.

The Bible is an amazing book. Every year it is the best-selling piece of literature in the world; it so far outsells every other book that the people who compile the best-seller lists don't even include it.

The Bible is unique. For one thing, it was written by forty different people over a period of nearly two thousand years under the direction of one editor, the Holy Spirit. Some of the people who penned Scripture were highly educated; others had never been off the farm. A few were common fishermen. At least one writer was a doctor, one was a tax collector, several were government officials, but only a few were what we would consider professional theologians. Most of the writers never met or communicated with one another in any way.

Despite this incredible diversity of human writers, the Bible has a remarkable unity and coherence. To put that feat in perspective, imagine that you were able to pick out forty friends and ask them to write on religion, ethics, science, the creation of the world, the meaning of life, the end of the world. At times, their ideas would probably contradict each other. But the Bible's writers and subject matter flow together in an incredibly complimentary fashion. And in spite of the different time periods and cultures represented by the people who wrote the Bible, people today find hope and inspiration from its words.

But can you really believe the Bible? Sure you can. Jesus did. He quoted from twenty-four separate books of the Old Testament, confirming its authority. History, archeology, and scientific evidence also continue to authenticate the Bible's accuracy. Hundreds of fulfilled prophecies (historically verifiable) support the veracity of God's Word. The Bible continues to be confirmed through its power to transform lives today.

So study the Word with confidence. As the Scriptures become part of your everyday life, your thoughts, your conversations, and your decision making, you will be pleasantly surprised at how the Holy Spirit uses the Word of God to be your personal "On Course Instructor." No batteries required.

PRAYER
Dozens of important decisions face me every day.
Father, help me to discover the direction
I need through Your Word.

FURTHER READING
2 Timothy 3:13–17; 2 Peter 1:20–21; Matthew 5:18

PLAYING DIRTY

Brethren, even if a man is caught in any trespass,
you who are spiritual,
restore such a one in a spirit of gentleness;
each one looking to yourself, lest you too be tempted.
GALATIANS 6:1

PGA pro Mark Calcavecchia was playing well, feeling good, and he was looking good, too. He was in contention on the sixth hole of the 1986 Kemper Open at the TPC Avenel Course in Potomac, Maryland, when he misplayed a shot and drove the ball into a ravine. Undeterred, Mark climbed down the hill to reach his ball, but the steep ravine became Mark's great undoing.

As he attempted to take a step to determine whether he

could play the ball where it was lying, Mark slipped and fell *splat* into a mud puddle. His clothes were covered with mud. At first, the spectators and commentators held their breath and watched in silence, until someone discovered that Mark had suffered no physical injuries. Then the snickers started, and before long, the chuckles turned to outright belly laughter.

By the time Calcavecchia was able to extricate himself from the muddy mess, he was soaked and disgusted. His game went downhill from there. Still caked with mud, he withdrew from the tournament a few holes later.

Stumbling and falling. It happens all the time in the spiritual realm. Sometimes it hurts, other times it is merely frustrating and embarrassing, but it is always a tragedy. And the reaction of our superpious friends is often the same as the crowd that observed Mark Calcavecchia's calamity: "Oh, you're hurting? You've fallen? I really didn't notice," they say as they step over us, perhaps kicking us again as they go by.

In Galatians 6:1, the apostle Paul said we should have a different attitude toward our Christian brothers and sisters who fall down or get messed up. If you have fallen lately, let these words of restoration be a comfort. If you know someone else who has gotten caught in a trespass, let these words be a challenge. Paul's instruction is clear: Be gentle in restoring your brothers and sisters when they fall because the next person to get in a mess might just be you.

To slip and fall in our attempts to please God is nothing new. Paul reminded us that "all have sinned and fall short of the glory of God" (Romans 3:23). So let's not play any self-righteous, spiritual games. God doesn't get nearly so angry when we stumble and fall so long as we are stumbling in His direction. If we simply call upon Him for help, He will patiently pick us up, brush us off, lovingly discipline us if necessary, and then put us on the right path again.

But if we choose to walk in disobedience, willfully continuing to walk contrary to His direction, we're on our own. And we know where that road will take us.

Today, choose to take Paul's advice seriously. Be gentle with yourself and with your brothers and sisters.

PRAYER

Father, I know what it feels like to fall and make a mess of things. Please forgive me for my failures, my mistakes, and my sins. And help me to be compassionate toward others who slip along the way. May I be able to offer a helping hand to get them back on their feet again.

FURTHER READING
Galatians 6:1–16

FAMILY FIRST

For this cause a man shall leave his father and his mother,
and shall cleave to his wife;
and they shall become one flesh.
GENESIS 2:24

Over the years, there have been plenty of books written about golf: biographies of great players, how-to's about every aspect of the game, as well as jokes, quips, and quote books concerning life on the links. The first woman to write a book about golf was Mrs. Edward Kennard, who penned *The Sorrows of a Golfer's Wife.* The year? 1896.

Mrs. Kennard was expressing a perennial problem: Tension can exist between our love for golf and our love for our family. The wise person will keep a proper balance between those two interests. Keep this in mind, though: When we stand before God on Judgment Day, He will not be examining our golf scores. He will look very carefully at how we dealt with our family.

Marriage is not simply an institution of society, and "family values" is not merely an overworked and under-lived political slogan. God created Adam and Eve and performed the first marriage ceremony, bringing them together as husband and wife and starting the first family.

Children, too, are spoken of in Scripture as being a blessing from the Lord. Some of the most beloved accounts in the Bible revolve around a husband and wife who could not have children but then, as a sign of the blessing of God, conceived, sometimes miraculously. Abraham and Sarah (Genesis 16:1), Hannah and Elkanah (1 Samuel 1:2), and Zacharias and Elizabeth, parents of John the Baptist (Luke 1:5–7), are examples.

Solomon, said to be the wisest man who ever lived, unreservedly declared: "Behold, children are a gift of the LORD; the fruit of the womb is a reward. Like arrows in the hand of a warrior, so are the children of one's youth. How blessed is the man whose quiver is full of them; they shall not be ashamed, when they speak with their enemies in the gate" (Psalm 127:3–5).

Notice, Solomon likens kids to arrows in a warrior's hand; the quiver to which he refers is the warrior's arrow case. The average quiver in biblical times could hold five or more arrows. Now, that's enough to make you really quiver!

God is definitely pro-family. And if God is such an enthusiastic supporter of family life, shouldn't we be too? Nothing—not even our golf game!—should take priority over our families.

PRAYER
Lord, You have given me my family to help me
discover what it means to be part of Your family.
Show me Your priorities,
and help me to balance my responsibilities in the workplace,
the community, my church, and yes,
even my time on the golf course,
with the time allotted for my family.

FURTHER READING
1 Timothy 4:1–3; Hebrews 13:4;
Matthew 19:6; Colossians 3:12–21

CHRISTIANS AT
THE MASTERS

Now the God of peace. . .
equip you in every good thing to do His will,
working in us that which is pleasing in His sight,
through Jesus Christ,
to whom be the glory forever and ever. Amen.
HEBREWS 13:20–21

The Masters Tournament, held each year at Augusta National Golf Club, is known for many things—Tiger Woods's youthful victory, Greg Norman's astonishing collapse, forty-six-year-old Jack Nicklaus's sixth title. For nearly a century, one family has chronicled many of the great Masters' moments on film. Three generations of "Christians"—as in the Frank Christian family —have photographed the high points and low points at the annual Augusta National pilgrimage.

Now in his early sixties, Frank Christian, Jr. has been the official tournament photographer at the Masters for more than forty years. His shots deck the walls of golf aficionados around the world. He has photographed all the greats. His un-flattering shot of Arnold Palmer and Ben Hogan with gruff expressions on their faces and cigarettes dangling from their mouths while waiting on the second tee in 1966 is a golf classic. Another of Christian's photos that caught the emotion of the Masters was his shot of Jack Nicklaus being kissed by his wife and sister following his Masters win in 1986.

To Frank Christian, all the shots are special. "When you're documenting history, it's hard to say this moment or this picture [is] more important to me," he said. "There's a unique story behind them all."[1]

One key ingredient to Christian's success as a photographer is his attention to detail in the developing process. After all, it's one thing to focus your subject in the lens of your camera. It's another to be able to take a great snapshot. But if you neglect the developing process, all your efforts will be in vain. Have you ever seen photographs printed from film that was allowed to remain undeveloped for too long? They may have been great shots when they were first taken, but if not acted upon, they turn a pale, dingy yellow. The photo is ruined, wasted, lost.

The developing process itself is interesting. A photographer's darkroom is illuminated by a red light that casts an unusual pall over the place. The photographer's workbench is lined with trays filled with developing solutions, and the space above the developing trays is usually cluttered with already developed photographs hanging up to dry. Gazing at the mess, the uninitiated might decide, *Maybe I'd better take my film to a one-hour processing place!*

The developer knows, however, that great photographs cannot be rushed. Each step of the process is somewhat messy and requires special attention. The latent images in the camera must first be made into negatives. Then the negatives are used to produce the prints. The process involves the careful application of just the right amounts of chemical solutions:

- alkaline and acidic rinses, which turn the images on film into actual pictures the world can see;
- fixing solutions, which cause photo images to stabilize and remain intact on the paper; and

- washing solutions, which thoroughly cleanse the paper and prevent water spots and streaks on finished photos.

If any part of the developing process is ignored, forgotten, or circumvented, the quality of the photo is jeopardized. Regardless of the fantastic images on the film, if we don't allow time for proper development, we could easily end up with a blank roll of film, good for nothing but pitching into the garbage.

In many ways, our lives are similar to photographs. Just as a photograph is a reproduction and reminder of the original experience, our lives are reproductions and reminders of Jesus. We are called not only to experience Christ for ourselves, but to represent Him to everyone who views our lives. A photograph requires proper development if it is going to be a quality reproduction of the original; the same is true of our lives.

God is taking the raw film of our lives and turning the negatives into positive prints—His prints—intended to reflect His glory. Sometimes the "alkaline rinse" stings as He exposes hidden images and brings them to the surface in our lives. At times the "acidic rinse" causes us to cringe and squirm in discomfort and doubt as God strips away the impurities that might blur the reflection of His image in us. But through it all,

He is carefully conducting the process. He is developing us, washing us with the water of His Word, "that He might present to Himself the church in all her glory, having no spot or wrinkle or any such thing; but that she should be holy and blameless" (Ephesians 5:27).

Rest assured, not only has there been a Christian at work at the Masters, the Master has been at work on the Christians.

PRAYER
Father, sometimes it is difficult for me to
understand the process You are using
to develop Your reflection in me.
Increase my faith, O Lord,
to trust that Your will for me is good,
that Your plan is to make positive prints
out of my negatives,
and that through it all,
the world will see Jesus in me.

FURTHER READING
Philippians 3:10–14

DON'T WORRY, BE HAPPY

Therefore do not be anxious for tomorrow;
for tomorrow will care for itself.
Each day has enough trouble of its own.
MATTHEW 6:34

It's nearly impossible to play golf well and worry at the same time. Worry is a robber. It interferes with our thought processes, our emotions, and our physical well-being. It causes us to become tense and stressed out—and stressed-out golfers are high handicappers.

Worry on the golf course paralyzes us. It robs us of our ability to focus on our game. It destroys concentration and saps our ability to perform. Rather than worry about what might happen in the future, or even what has happened in the past, we'd be much better off to focus on the immediate shot.

To play golf well takes practice. Doing it right, hitting good shots, knowing that we did it, and being able to do it again on a regular basis—that's what good golf is all about. But that takes time to develop. Often, we fret and worry our way around the course: "Can I really carry that pond? Do I have enough club to make that green?" This makes our minds reluctant to send the message to the body that will produce consistently good golf shots. We must practice each bit of instruction until it becomes second nature, until we can do the right thing automatically. Once we do, our bodies will let us know that it is right, and the results on the course will bear witness, as well.

The Christian life is similar. It is impossible to trust God and worry at the same time. That doesn't mean that we will go through life as eternal optimists, nor does it mean we should not make wise plans and set realistic goals. It does mean, however, that the Lord has promised to take care of us if we will only trust Him. If we allow worry to overshadow everything we do, we will be stymied in our efforts to live victoriously. On the other hand, if we learn to trust the Lord with the details of our lives, we will discover incredible freedom.

The psalmist gave us a wonderful pattern to incorporate into our lives:

Trust in the LORD, and do good;
Dwell in the land and cultivate faithfulness.
Delight yourself in the LORD;
And He will give you the desires of your heart.
Commit your way to the LORD,
Trust also in Him, and He will do it.

PSALM 37:3–5

Notice the active verbs in his advice: Trust, dwell, delight, commit, and trust some more! Rather than worry, try trust. As you do, trust will lead you not only to transitory happiness, but more importantly it will lead to eternal joy.

PRAYER

Lord, at times it's easier to worry than it is to trust.
But by an act of my will,
today I choose to trust You rather than to worry.

FURTHER READING
Proverbs 3:5–6

ROLLING 'EM STRAIGHT

And let endurance have its perfect result,
that you may be perfect and complete, lacking in nothing.
But if any of you lacks wisdom, let him ask of God,
who gives to all men generously and without reproach,
and it will be given to him.
But let him ask in faith without any doubting,
for the one who doubts is like the surf of
the sea driven and tossed by the wind.
For let not that man expect that he will receive
anything from the Lord,
being a double-minded man,
unstable in all his ways.
JAMES 1:4–8

Every golfer knows that the short putt counts just as much on the scorecard as the long drive off the tee. You can crunch the ball on the fairway, hit the green in regulation, but if your putts are not rolling into the hole, the scorecard will show it. Sometimes, though, it seems that no matter what you do, the ball refuses to roll straight or to drop in the cup. When that happens, your confidence shatters. That's what happened to Tom Watson.

A six-time PGA Player of the Year, five-time leading money winner, holder of eight major championships, and captain of the 1993 American Ryder Cup Team, Tom Watson went through a long period in which his poor putting cost him one tournament after another. At the 1994 AT&T Tournament, Tom was at the top of the leader board in the final round when he three-putted one of the last holes, allowing Johnny Miller to win. That same year, Watson was in contention to win the Masters, the U.S. Open, and the British Open, but his putter let him down during the final round in each tournament.

Frustrated but unwilling to give up, Tom Watson tried everything he knew to get his putts to roll straight. He changed the grip on his putter—several times—changed putters, changed his stance, and tried to change his thoughts as he stood over putts. Nothing helped. Before long, Tom's confidence began to wobble. By 1995, Watson was clearly shaken.

"There's an element of doubt when I stand over a putt," Tom said at the close of the season. "It's an awful thing. But it comes from missing a lot of putts."[2]

Watson wasn't the only one who was doubting. Most spectators and commentators worried aloud whenever Tom approached a green. They cringed every time Tom slumped over his putter as another ball spun away from the hole, stopped short, or trickled a few inches past the cup.

With fragile faith, Tom Watson continued fighting his putting fears throughout the first part of the 1996 season. He had a chance to win in New Orleans, but he bogied four straight holes on the final nine, most of the strokes racking up on the green. He missed the cut at the Masters, a failure Tom Watson had never before experienced in his professional career.

At the Memorial in Dublin, Ohio, a tournament hosted by Jack Nicklaus—the man Tom had beaten in the 1977 British Open as well as the 1977 Masters and the 1982 British Open—Watson shot a 70, 68, and a 66 to take a one-stroke lead into the final round. Nearly everyone in the gallery thought that Tom would blow the tournament with his putter.

The last day of the tournament, Tom made a tough four-foot putt early in the day on number five. He also made a twelve-footer for birdie on number ten, and he still led by three strokes when he approached the fifteenth hole. Then

Tom lived down to everyone's expectations. He botched a four-foot pressure putt on fifteen.

This time, however, Watson was not about to lose his cool. He parred the next two holes and then put his approach shot to within fourteen feet on number eighteen. As Watson walked onto the eighteenth green, the crowd greeted him with a thunderous roar of applause and cheers. Watson rolled in the final putt for birdie, defeating David Duval by two strokes.

It's not always easy to keep things rolling straight. Sometimes it seems that our prayers are bouncing off the ceiling, deflected back in our faces, almost taunting us with their lack of effectiveness. But we cannot give up. We must keep on believing, keep going to God with confidence not in our ability to perform, but in His ability to answer our prayers in the way that is best for us.

PRAYER
Lord, I am going to trust You and believe Your Word,
even when it seems that nothing is going my way.
I know that You are true,
that You hear and will answer my prayers.

FURTHER READING
Psalm 139:23–24

YOU GOTTA PLAY
BY THE RULES

Be diligent to present yourself approved to God
as a workman who does not need to be ashamed,
handling accurately the word of truth.
2 TIMOTHY 2:15

At the March 1997 Players Championship, Davis Love III, one of the top players on the PGA Tour, did the unthinkable: He blew a tournament because he ignored the rules of golf. At the seventeenth green during the final round, Davis was taking a practice stroke on a six-foot putt that would have pushed him into the top five on the leader board when he inadvertently bumped the ball with the toe of his putter. The ball rolled to Love's right about eighteen inches.

According to the rules of golf, Davis should have moved the ball back to its original position and given himself a one-stroke penalty. He didn't. Instead, Love quickly putted out and walked off the green, thinking he had bogied the hole. Actually, he had double-bogied the hole, since he unknowingly had been assessed a two-stroke penalty for hitting his ball from the wrong location. Worse yet, when Love signed his scorecard, he was still unaware of his infraction. Because he turned in an incorrect score, he was disqualified from the tournament.

Consequently, Davis Love III not only lost approximately $100,000 in prize money that he would have won, but by being disqualified, he was not eligible for any pay at all—a week's worth of work for nothing.

Commenting on his blunder, Davis said later, "When I saw what I had done [by hitting the ball unintentionally], I think my mind blanked out. I was standing there thinking, 'There's no way I did what I just did.' My immediate reaction was just to go over and putt out, get out of there as fast as I could because I was so embarrassed."[3]

Most of us make mistakes in life, some of which are costly and embarrassing, but ignorance is not always bliss, nor is it an acceptable excuse. Davis Love III's ignorance of one of the rules of golf cost him a tournament purse, but ignorance of the Rules of Life, God's Word, can be deadly.

Many of us who say we live according to the Bible can't recite even a few of the Ten Commandments or the Beatitudes. The truth is, we need to read the Bible regularly, every day if possible. It nourishes our souls just as food strengthens our bodies. Beyond mere reading, we need to study the Scriptures, to learn the rules, to ponder their meaning, and then make use of them in our daily lives.

It's important to allow the Bible to speak for itself. We don't need to search for strange, obscure, hidden nuggets from the Word. As Mark Twain said, "It's not the things I don't understand about the Bible that bother me; it's the things I do understand that bother me."[4] Concentrate on what you comprehend, and the Lord will continue to expand your understanding.

As you study the Scriptures, read the various books and letters in the Bible as you would any other exciting book or important document. Don't skip around aimlessly, using the Bible as a horoscope, hoping to find some direction for the day. Study the Scriptures systematically, and you will be surprised how much specific instruction you discover for each day.

Most important of all, respond to what God is saying to you through His Word. The Bible is God's Rule Book, but it is also His love letter to you. Allow Him to speak to your heart and mind, and then do what His Word says.

PRAYER
Teach me, Lord, the things I need to know
to correctly play the "game of life."
May your Word be not only the Rule Book,
but my Guidebook, as well.

FURTHER READING
Psalm 19:7–8; Psalm 119:64; James 1:19–27

A TEE TIME
YOU DON'T WANT TO MISS

Take heed, keep on the alert;
for you do not know when the appointed time is.
Mark 13:33

Have you ever missed a tee time because you didn't get to the course on time? If so, you are in good company. The great Spanish golfer Seve Ballesteros was disqualified from the 1980 U.S. Open because he arrived late at the first tee. Seve's excuse? He was tied up in traffic. Most tournament officials as well as club starters take a dim view of missed tee times.

When it comes to missing the time Jesus talked about—

the day of the Lord's return—we dare not be late. Jesus was quite emphatic that He would return to earth. In Matthew 24, we can read some of the "signs of the times" Jesus told His disciples to watch for—signs that would indicate that His coming is near. Some of the cataclysmic events that Jesus predicted include wars, famines, earthquakes, the rise of false prophets, increased lawlessness, and a falling away of many believers. On a more positive note, Jesus also said that the gospel would be preached in all the world before He returns to earth.

Making matters a bit more complicated, Jesus said nobody knows just when He will be coming back for us. He said to be ready to go at a moment's notice, to keep our hearts right with Him so we will be ready when He appears.

How are we supposed to do that? If we are living in the last days, as many Bible scholars believe, what should our attitudes and lifestyles be, and what should be at the top of our priority lists?

Apparently, these were some of the questions on the apostle Peter's mind as he penned his second letter to the early Christian churches. In 2 Peter 3, Peter gave us at least six principles by which to live.

1. He told us to keep "looking for and hastening the coming of the day of God" (v. 12). In other

words, keep watching for the Lord's return and the judgment of God to be poured out upon the earth. Peter said, "You know it is coming. Keep your eyes open! Keep looking for that day."

Watching and waiting we understand, but what does the apostle mean by our "hastening the day"? How can we hurry God? We can't. It's foolish to even try to do so. But, we "hasten the day of God" by taking the gospel to our world, by revealing the truth that Jesus is this world's only hope of salvation.

We need to see our world as Jesus sees it—on a collision course with destruction—and allow that knowledge to motivate us to share the message of salvation with those around us.

2. Peter prompted us to "be diligent to be found by Him in peace, spotless and blameless" (v. 14). That means that our hearts and minds are clean before God, that we have repented of every known sin we have committed. Think of it this way: In a beautiful wedding, the bride doesn't come down the aisle in a filthy dress. She wears the most gorgeous gown she can afford. Her dress symbolizes the things Peter

mentions: peace, spotlessness, blamelessness—
in a word, purity.

3. Peter told us to "regard the patience of our Lord
to be salvation" (v. 15). The Lord is patiently
providing people an opportunity to be saved
from the destruction to come and to be saved to
a relationship with Jesus. Now is the time to
establish such a relationship, not when we hear
the sound of the heavenly trumpet. Peter
warned us that God's patience is balanced by
His promise; He will follow through on His
Word, and the prophecies will come to pass
(v. 9). Still, God doesn't want anyone to perish,
and He is patiently allowing people a little more
time to hear the gospel and to repent. With this
in mind, what are we doing to help our friends
and family prepare for that day?

4. Peter reminded us to "be on your guard"
(v. 17). This is a caution against being led
astray or falling away from the Lord. We're too
close to home to slack off now. This is no time
to be lazy in our spiritual disciplines.

5. We are to "grow in the grace and knowledge of our Lord and Savior Jesus Christ" (v. 18). Our goal should be for our character to grow more like that of Jesus every day.

6. Finally, Peter encouraged us to give God the glory, "now and to the day of eternity" (v. 18). That is the ultimate purpose of the Christian life.

If we practice what the apostle Peter preached, we will not only avoid missing our starting time with God, but we will encourage others to be ready to meet Him on that day as well.

PRAYER
May I live each day with the excitement and expectation
that this might be the day I meet You face-to-face.
Let Your eternal perspective, O Lord,
be the standard by which I view the everyday events
in which I am involved.

FURTHER READING
Matthew 24:1–44; 1 Thessalonians 4:13–18

BASEBALL POWER
OR CLUB-HEAD SPEED

"This is the word of the LORD to Zerubbabel saying,
'Not by might, nor by power, but by My Spirit,
says the LORD of hosts.' "
ZECHARIAH 4:6

In case you haven't already noticed, hitting a golf ball is a lot different from hitting a baseball. In baseball, we can use brute strength in our upper body to power the ball out of the park. If we try to hit a golf ball the same way, we quickly discover that a power swing simply doesn't work. At times, swinging too hard causes us to whiff, missing the ball completely. Is there anything more frustrating and embarrassing than to stand with club in hands and miss that little ball?

To strike a golf ball well, we must start off from a position of zero tension, coil up like a spring by turning our hips to the right until our back pocket faces the target, and then unleash, whipping the club with such centrifugal force that it blasts that little white ball into oblivion (or at least a good distance down the fairway). The more smoothly we swing, the more quickly our hips turn, the faster the club head moves, the more squarely our club makes contact with the ball, and the better our shot. Simple, isn't it?

But it is not mere physical strength that provides the powerful impact; it is allowing the physical attribute of the golf club, as designed by the manufacturer, to do what it was created to do. That's why a big, 250-pound lummox can swing like a maniac and merely dribble the ball off the tee, while a slightly built PGA Senior Tour player such as the 125-pound Chi-Chi Rodriguez or a diminutive little woman such as LPGA star Anika Sorenstam can send the ball sailing.

Many amateur golfers make the mistake of trying to smash the ball as though they are Mark McGuire or Sammy Sosa gunning for a home-run record. They stand up to the ball with their feet wide apart, hold the club over their head, and then swing for the upper decks. They huff and they puff and they work up a sweat, but the little white ball merely taunts them as it trickles down the fairway a few hundred feet.

Why? Because no matter how big or how strong we are, we cannot hit a golf ball with sheer power and expect to achieve the same results as those players who obey the laws of physics and allow the golf club to operate according to the way the manufacturers designed it to perform—on the basis of club-head speed.

Something similar often occurs in our spiritual lives. We know where we want to go or what we want to accomplish. We see the goal in our sights. But all too often, we attempt to achieve spiritual power by exerting more human effort rather than by operating according to the Manufacturer's design. Our best efforts, regardless of how noble, will always fall short of the fairway, slice off the path into the rough, or hook into someone else's way.

It is easy to become discouraged at our inability to do what we know we ought to be doing. That sense of failure is heightened when we find ourselves doing those things God specifically says that He does not want us to be doing.

Such was the case during the time of the prophet Zechariah. Israel, God's people, had a knowledge of God that no other people around them possessed. They had experienced great miracles and knew that God was able to help them through their problems. Yet they turned their backs on Him and decided to do things their own way. When Israel rejected the truth and sinned, God punished them by allowing them to be carried away into slavery in Babylon. Years later, God's people repented, and the Lord forgave them. He sent a remnant of His people back to Jerusalem to rebuild the city and the holy temple.

The people returned with great enthusiasm. They immediately laid the foundation for the new projects, but then they ran into opposition from the local population. For the next eighteen years, not one stone was laid, not one bit of progress was made. The people became discouraged and disgruntled. Their high hopes and dreams were dashed. Eventually, they fell into the pattern of thinking, *Well, this must be the best we can expect.* Many of the people began feeling so sorry for themselves, they said, "God has forgotten us."

Into this situation God sent the prophet Zechariah to speak to His people. Zechariah's name was a message in itself; it means, "The Lord has remembered us."

Indeed, God had remembered His people. He had never forgotten them. He was allowing them to learn the difficult lesson each of us must discover for ourselves: We cannot live a holy life under our own power. God—our Manufacturer— promised His people through Zechariah that they would be able to accomplish what He had called them to do, but it would not be through their own intellect, physical prowess, or ingenuity. Zechariah's message is still relevant: "God has remembered you. He is going to make you a light to the world, but it will not be through your might; not through your power, but the work will be done by the Spirit of the Lord!"

PRAYER

*Father, I have been trying to do Your work
and Your will under my own might and power.
I admit my inability to get the job done
through human energies,
and I ask You to let the power
of Your Spirit flow through me,
so Your work can be accomplished
in Your way and for Your glory.*

FURTHER READING
Zechariah 4:1–6

WHAT COMES NATURALLY

For the good that I wish, I do not do;
but I practice the very evil that I do not wish.
ROMANS 7:19

Whoever said that the golf swing is a natural motion must have been speaking tongue in cheek. Few motions in sports are actually as unnatural as the golf swing. To generate power, you must stand to the side of the ball, unable to face your target the way you can in other sports such as football, basketball, baseball, or tiddlywinks. As you prepare to swing, your eyes and brain both seem to want to work against you. To make matters worse, your first move is away from your target! All the while, a little voice in your head is taunting, *There's no way you are going to hit that ball when your body is twisted around so unnaturally.*

Even the way you grip a golf club is diametrically opposed to the way you'd hold nearly any other object of approximately the same size, shape, and substance. Can you imagine, for instance, using the interlocking grip on a hammer or a broom? Try to use the Vardon grip—as unnatural a hand position as ever invented in which the pinky finger of the right hand overlaps the first and second fingers of the left hand—to cast a fishing pole or swing a hockey stick. Nope, there's nothing natural about golf alignment, and what comes naturally usually won't bring about the desired results.

Maybe we shouldn't be so surprised. After all, when it comes to spiritual things, what comes naturally is usually not in our best interests. Left to pursue our natural inclinations, we would soon discover that those inclinations yield disastrous results. Yet if we are honest with ourselves, we must admit that often doing what comes naturally has tremendous appeal.

In the Disney made-for-adults animated movie *Who Framed Roger Rabbit?* Jessica, the voluptuous vixen, purrs to drooling private detective Eddie Valiant, "I'm not bad; I'm just drawn that way."

Have you ever felt like that? You keep telling yourself that you don't really want to do that sinful thing, get into that compromising position, go to that place, think those thoughts, or say those words. Yet you find yourself inevitably sliding toward sin. Why is that?

Part of the answer is that we are born in sin. Not that there is anything sinful about birth itself, but we were born into a world of sin. Moreover, we were born with inherently sinful attitudes. Think about it: Nobody has to teach a child to be bad. It comes naturally. Most parents don't sit down with their children and instruct, "Now, here's how you become a selfish person." We pick that characteristic up quite well on our own!

That's why Jessica's assessment of her situation is partially true. From the day we are born, we are drawn toward bad things. But veiled behind Jessica's statement is a subtle temptation to blame her "badness" on her creator. That's nothing new, either. Down through history, men and women have sought to excuse their sinful tendencies by blaming somebody or something else.

It started with Adam and Eve. Adam knew what God had said about not eating a particular fruit in the Garden of Eden. But when Eve showed Adam the tantalizing fruit, it looked so-o-o good! Adam could imagine how it would feel to hold it in his hand, to taste it with his tongue, to feel the moist juices sliding down his throat. The fruit probably had a pleasant fragrance as well.

As Adam's senses were aroused, all of God's words seemed to go out the window. He wanted what he wanted, and he wanted it now. That's basic lust.

God asked him the probing question, "Have you eaten from the tree of which I commanded you not to eat?" (Genesis 3:11). In response, Adam waffled: "The woman whom Thou gavest to be with me, she gave me from the tree, and I ate" (3:12). Besides skewering his wife, notice Adam's subtle inference that this whole matter might be God's fault: "After all, Lord, You put me together with that woman, and I mean, I was just doing what came naturally!" Sounds a lot like Jessica, doesn't it?

Eve's response was no better. When the Lord asked her for an explanation, she used the serpent as an excuse: "The serpent deceived me, and I ate" (3:13). Most of us tend to look for excuses when we succumb to temptations and decide to do what we know is wrong. We try to blame God, our parents, the environment in which we live, peer pressure, poor potty training, something! We'll do anything but admit that we are responsible for our actions.

But the Bible makes it clear that we sin because we want to.

Only Jesus can give us the power to choose right over

wrong. Oh, sure, we might be good for goodness' sake. . .for a while. When temptation comes, especially temptation to seek that which satisfies our self-interests, inevitably we give in. We're only human.

But Jesus Christ is God. He is more than human! With His power working in us, saying no to what is wrong and saying yes to what is right is not only possible, it is enjoyable!

PRAYER

Lord, I know all too well my own weaknesses.
But Your Word tells me that where I am weak, You are strong.
Please rule in my life to the extent that
my battles with temptations are not fought with human
energy, ingenuity, or my own ability to overcome,
but in the power of Your Word
and with the help of Your Holy Spirit.

FURTHER READING
Genesis 3:1–24; Romans 7:6–8:6

NOW THAT'S A
LOUSY SHOT!

And the blood of Jesus His Son
cleanses us from all sin.
1 JOHN 1:7

Bobby P. (name withheld to protect the guilty) dubbed a five-iron shot and beaned his buddy's mom while she was sitting in a golf cart. Steve A. sliced while hitting his drive off a tee parallel to a highway. The ball streaked through the sky, found an opening in the trees, and smashed into the windshield of an oncoming car. Marc C. hit a powerful knock-down tee shot on a narrow fairway lined with expensive homes on both sides. Unfortunately, Marc's shot zoomed too far left and crashed through the window of one of the homes, landing on the dining-room table just as the family was sitting down to dinner.

Perhaps the worst shot to which anyone will admit was struck by Mathieu Boya, an avid golfer in Benin, a small country in Africa. In 1987, Benin did not have a golf course, but that did not keep Mathieu from practicing his game. He regularly practiced hitting golf balls in an open field next to the Benin Air Base.

One day, Boya hit an errant shot off the tee. The ball struck a bird which happened to be flying over the air base. The stunned bird fell into the open cockpit of a fighter jet which was on the runway and about to take off. The bird—still alive—so surprised the pilot of the jet that he lost control of his plane and crashed into four Mirage jets that were parked on the runway, thus in one fell swoop wiping out the entire Benin Air Force. All five planes were destroyed, and the pilot barely escaped with his life. When the damages were totaled, Boya's errant drive cost in excess of $40 million. Now, that's a lousy shot!

Many people feel that they cannot approach God because they have had too many bad shots in life; they have done too many things wrong; their sin is too great. Nothing could be farther from the truth.

We have all sinned and fallen short of the glory of God. We've all missed the mark and gone down a few wrong paths —some of us a lot more than a few! The degree of sin is not the important matter, however. There is no such thing as a big sin or a little sin in God's book. The angels don't sit in heaven keeping score: "Let's see, that's three marks against Bobby P. for beaning his buddy's mom; ten marks against Marc C. for destroying that family's dining-room window, not to mention their dinner. And, oh, boy, that's a big one hundred for Mathieu Boya!"

It doesn't work that way. In God's book, sin is sin, and all sin is equally repulsive to Him. Every sin carries with it the potential to ruin our lives and to destroy our relationship with God forever. The fact that other people have done worse things than we have or that we have done worse things than they is irrelevant. The fact that everybody else is bogged down with some sort of sinful baggage doesn't lessen the burden or relieve the pangs of guilt we experience.

The Bible makes it clear that there is only one remedy for sin. It does not lie in a vain attempt to forget our past or to excuse our failures. The remedy to sin lies in a personal relationship with Jesus Christ, in receiving His forgiveness and transforming power in our lives. Here is the good news about sin:

But now God has shown us a different way to heaven—not by "being good enough" and trying to keep his laws, but by a new way (though not new, really, for the Scriptures told about it long ago). Now God says he will accept and acquit us—declare us "not guilty"—if we trust Jesus Christ to take away our sins. And we all can be saved in this same way, by coming to Christ, no matter who we are or what we have been like.

Romans 3:21–22 tlb

When we honestly confess our sins to the Lord, He forgives. Ugly sins, dark sins, areas of our lives that nobody else knows about or could even imagine—He forgives them all. And He allows us to start again, no matter the size of our infractions or the repercussions they have caused. That's not to say that there will be no consequences for our sins. We may still have to pay for the broken window, but the sin is gone, forgiven, washed in the blood of Christ.

If there were no other reason for being a Christian (and there are many!), the forgiveness and release from guilt we experience when we meet Jesus would be rationale enough.

PRAYER

Thank You, Lord, that the cleansing power
of Your blood goes far deeper than my sin.
Let me be ever conscious of the price You paid
for my freedom and forgiveness of sin,
and let that awareness motivate me to say no
to those things that are wrong
and yes to those things that honor You.

FURTHER READING
Romans 6

YOUR GOOD—
GOD'S GLORY

And we know that God causes
all things to work together
for good to those who love God,
to those who are called
according to His purpose.
ROMANS 8:28

One of the keys to enjoying your golf game is confidence. Having confidence does not necessarily mean that every shot is going to be knockdown perfect. Nor does it mean that every round of golf is going to be our best. Ben Crenshaw, 1995

Masters Champion, described the tenuous balance between confidence and golf when he said, "Golf is the hardest game in the world. There's no way you can ever get it. Just when you think you do, the game jumps up and puts you into your place."[5]

Obviously, confidence on the golf course does not demand perfection. But confidence implies that even when things aren't going our way, we know that there is purpose, direction, and value in what we are doing. We can be confident as Christians because we know that God is in control. Though the outlook may be temporarily gloomy or circumstances may be difficult, we can rest assured that God is working out all things for our good and His glory.

In a fascinating account recorded in three separate places in Scripture (2 Kings 18–19; 2 Chronicles 32:1–23; and Isaiah 36–37), God's people, led by King Hezekiah, faced dire circumstances. They were being held under siege by King Sennacherib of Assyria. The enemy had already seized all the major fortified cities of Judah, and the Assyrians were now putting heavy pressure on Jerusalem, the capital city. Sennacherib demanded a hefty ransom from God's people and then sent his emissary Rabshakeh to intimidate Hezekiah into making a deal. Each day Rabshakeh stood outside the city walls, yelling insults toward Hezekiah, toward God, and toward God's people.

When King Hezekiah heard Rabshakeh's words, he tore his clothes and covered himself with sackcloth as signs of both his heartrending grief and his humility before God. Then Hezekiah went into the house of the Lord to pray.

No doubt, had Hezekiah thrown up his hands in despair, the battle would have been all over for God's people. But Hezekiah didn't do that. Instead he submitted to God, and he testified of God's greatness. He resisted the enemy by refusing to respond in foolish verbal confrontations, and then he diffused the enemy's threats by taking them to the Lord in prayer. Hezekiah didn't begin outlining his woeful dilemma to God. He began by praising God. He said, "O LORD, the God of Israel, who art enthroned above the cherubim, Thou art the God, Thou alone, of all the kingdoms of the earth. Thou hast made heaven and earth" (2 Kings 19:15).

Isn't that a marvelous picture? With the devil beating on his door, Hezekiah paused to praise the Lord and testify of His awesome power before asking Him for help. Then he sent for the prophet Isaiah, hoping that Isaiah would have a word from the Lord.

Isaiah did. He told Hezekiah's emissaries to tell the king, "Thus says the LORD, 'Do not be afraid because of the words that you have heard, with which the servants of the king of Assyria have blasphemed Me. Behold, I will put a spirit in him so that he shall hear a rumor and return to his own land. And I will make him fall by the sword in his own land' " (Isaiah 37:6–7).

Shortly after this, Sennacherib mysteriously received word that Babylon was in rebellion. He abandoned his siege of Jerusalem and headed his army homeward. But God wasn't finished with Sennacherib. Nobody blasphemes Almighty God and gets away with it for long.

"Then the angel of the LORD went out, and struck 185,000 in the camp of the Assyrians; and when men arose early in the morning, behold, all of these were dead" (Isaiah 37:36). If you ever have any doubt about how strong the angel of the Lord is, let this account cause faith to well up in your heart. One angel destroyed 185,000 of the devil's finest warriors overnight! The Bible says, "The angel of the LORD encamps around those who fear Him, and rescues them" (Psalm 34:7).

Sennacherib, the devil's man, returned home defeated, where he was eventually murdered by his own sons. Hezekiah and the people of God won a great victory by surrendering the battle to the Lord.

When circumstances seem bleak, remember our God is still Almighty. Let your confidence be in Him.

PRAYER

Your power, O God, is awesome.
You are the only one true God,
and I will praise You no matter what
the circumstances of my life.
You are worthy of my praise,
and I will not allow the voices around me
to stifle that which pleases You.

FURTHER READING

2 Chronicles 32:1–23; 1 John 5:13–14

MR. PRESSURE

For momentary, light affliction is producing for us
an eternal weight of glory far beyond all comparison.
2 CORINTHIANS 4:17

Raymond Floyd is the type of fellow who likes to eat stress with a spatula. Even-tempered, easygoing, and relaxed as a hibernating bear, Raymond Floyd is the epitome of the cool cucumber on the course. He has been accused of having ice water running through his veins.

Back in Miami, the walls of Raymond's den in his $2 million home are decorated with dozens of magazine covers bearing his image. In large trophy cases, Floyd displays the treasures he has won in tournaments over the years—including the Masters; the PGA, which he has won twice; and the Tournament Players Championship.

For years, however, one trophy eluded his grasp—the trophy that is presented to the winner of the U.S. Open. With the exception of perhaps Sam Snead, no player of Floyd's "Hall of Fame" status had posted a more disheartening series of performances at this premier golf event. Not only had he not won the U.S. Open, Raymond rarely even placed in the top ten at that tournament. Although Raymond Floyd had won more than $3 million playing professional golf, very little of that money came from the U.S. Open. In twenty-one Opens, he won little more than $50 thousand.

Floyd remained nonplused about the absent trophy. "My philosophy," he said, "has always been: 'What difference does it make? If you play every week, you're going to have bad days, too. I think that's why I have the reputation for playing well under pressure."[6]

Indeed, the man can work under stress. At age forty-three, Raymond Floyd became the oldest man ever to win the U.S. Open.

The Scriptures tell us of another man who knew what it was like to live and work with stress. The man could have used a spiritual bulletproof vest. We know him today as the apostle Paul. Although there were times when Paul apparently had plenty of material comforts, other times were not so good. When he wrote to the Corinthians, he said of himself and his coworker Apollos, "To this present hour we are both hungry and thirsty, and are poorly clothed, and are roughly treated, and are homeless; and we toil, working with our own hands; when we are reviled, we bless; when we are persecuted, we endure; when we are slandered, we try to conciliate; we have become as the scum of the world, the dregs of all things, even until now" (1 Corinthians 4:11–13).

Paul was not living on easy street; his testimony was not that of a "King's Kid," at least not in the way that that concept has often been portrayed as "the prosperous Christian life." Quite the contrary, when Paul described himself and his closest associates, he said, "We are afflicted in every way, but not crushed; perplexed, but not despairing; persecuted, but not forsaken; struck down, but not destroyed; always carrying about in the body the dying of Jesus, that the life of Jesus also may be manifested in our body. For we who live are constantly being delivered over to death for Jesus' sake, that the life of Jesus also may be manifested in our mortal flesh" (2 Corinthians 4:8–11).

Hadn't Paul left all to follow Christ? Of course he had. Wasn't he an ideal candidate to receive tremendous blessings from God? It would seem that way to us. Funny, though, when Paul reviewed his Christian experience, he didn't mention anything about receiving a material blessing. Instead, he revealed that he had served God "in much endurance, in afflictions, in hardships, in distresses, in beatings, in imprisonments, in tumults, in labors, in sleeplessness, in hunger, . . .as sorrowful yet always rejoicing, as poor yet making many rich, as having nothing yet possessing all things" (2 Corinthians 6:4–5, 10).

In the same letter when compelled to defend his credentials as a true apostle, Paul recalled that he had been:

> Beaten times without number, often in danger of death. Five times I received from the Jews thirty-nine lashes. Three times I was beaten with rods, once I was stoned, three times I was shipwrecked, a night and a day I have spent in the deep. I have been on frequent journeys, in dangers from rivers, dangers from robbers, dangers from my countrymen, dangers from the Gentiles, dangers in the city, dangers in the wilderness, dangers on the sea, dangers among false brethren; I have been in labor and hardship, through many sleepless nights, in hunger and thirst, often without food, in cold and exposure. Apart from such external things, there is the daily pressure upon me of concern for all the churches.
>
> 2 CORINTHIANS 11:23–28

Ironically, rather than complaining that he had not lived a stress-free Christian life, Paul offered one of the most humble expressions of understatement in the Bible. He said, "Therefore we do not lose heart, but though our outer man is decaying, yet our inner man is being renewed day by day. For momentary, light affliction is producing for us an eternal weight of glory far beyond all comparison, while we look not at the things which are seen, but at the things which are not seen; for the things which are seen are temporal, but the things which are not seen are eternal" (2 Corinthians 4:16–18).

Did you catch that? Paul refers to the many tribulations he had endured for the sake of the gospel as "momentary, light afflictions." Talk about Mr. Pressure! The man knew how to deal with it. He kept his eyes on the eternal prize.

PRAYER

Father, You never promised that stress and pressure would be alleviated from my life. But when they come, please help me to handle them with Your grace. May I see the obstacles, inconveniences, and, yes, even the persecutions of this world as "momentary, light afflictions" in comparison to the eternal joy of knowing You.

FURTHER READING
Mark 10:28–30

REAL CONFIDENCE

Abide in Him,
so that when He appears, we may have confidence
and not shrink away from Him in shame at His coming.
1 JOHN 2:28

A recent survey of amateur golfers found that the average player shoots a 97 for eighteen holes. Only one third of all amateurs break 90 on a regular basis.[7] Surprised? You would be if you believed everything people say about their scorecards.

It's tempting to fudge on our scorecards, but it takes real confidence to honestly face the quality of our golf game. What good does it do to mark down a five when we know we really had a seven, eight, or higher? Who are we kidding, anyhow? If we are playing with some partners, they probably know we didn't have a five; after all, they saw us take two mulligans off the tee, fish a ball out of the pond with our $19.95 ball retriever, and blow three putts. To mark a five on the scorecard is not only a lie, it is an insult to the intelligence of our playing partners!

If we really want our golf game to improve (not to mention our prayer life), we need to start keeping score correctly. It's only by facing up to our bad shots on the golf course that we can resolve to do better next time, to do whatever it takes (including lessons, if necessary) to improve.

Never try to kid yourself into overlooking shots. Never tell yourself, *Well, that stroke didn't really count.* Come on. They all count! If we ignore strokes or simply don't count them, we are lying to ourselves. Who cares if our scorecard has a 39 on it for the front nine, when we know we really shot closer to 50?

So what if we streak into double numbers on the first hole or two? That's no excuse to quit keeping score. And do those automatic snowmen (8's) really do anything to improve our game? Sure, our partners are being gracious when they say, "Eight is as high as you can get on this course," but we know better because we've just proven that an eleven is extremely possible and, in fact, quite easily done.

Granted, it may blow our image as the next Tiger Woods or Hale Irwin (in case your age qualifies you for the Senior Tour) to pencil in a ten, eleven, or twelve on our card, but only by being truthful about our game will we ever find the resolve to do something about it.

On the other hand, don't be hard on yourself. Put in the larger context of the many challenges life brings, playing bogey golf isn't all that bad. Stop comparing yourself to others, and start enjoying your own game.

The same principle is true in our Christian walk. If we gauge ourselves by a Christian "superstar" (as if one really existed), we might think we are doing worse than we are. Conversely, if we look at Christians who have suffered severe failures in their lives, we may think, *Compared to them, I'm doing great!* In either case, we will probably be wrong. As Christians, our confidence is not in our own ability. Our confidence is in Christ Jesus. As we look at ourselves honestly, He will faithfully work in our lives to make us more like Him.

PRAYER

Father, help me to make an honest appraisal of myself, recognizing my strengths as well as my weaknesses, seeing Your gifts in my strengths and Your grace in my weaknesses. Remind me that in my weaknesses, You are strong.

FURTHER READING
Philippians 3:1–14

MURDER ON
THE GREEN

If we confess our sins,
He is faithful and righteous to forgive us our sins
and to cleanse us from all unrighteousness.
1 JOHN 1:9

Have you ever excitedly approached your ball on the green after a great shot, only to discover a crater right in your putting line? Somebody failed to repair a ball mark, and the resulting impression on the putting carpet produced a difficult shot for you and a nightmare repair job for the greenskeeper. Sadly, that mar on the green could easily have been corrected.

It takes a player five seconds to fix the average ball mark on a green. A properly repaired mark will heal in twenty-four hours, and the putting surface will look and roll as good as new. But if a player is ignorant of, or lazy about, the damage his or her ball makes and then neglects to repair it, within an hour, a mark on the green will leave a lasting scar. Left unattended, the grass will start to die. Even with the tender care of a talented greens-keeper, it will take an average of fifteen days for the grass to heal.

Ball marks on the green are an inevitable part of the game. They are going to happen. But unrepaired ball marks lead to the death and destruction of the greens we love.

Interestingly, sin in our lives is extremely similar to those ball marks. If we deal with our sin quickly, confessing it and asking forgiveness, it will still leave a mark, but healing and recovery will come much more quickly. When we confess, God forgives and He heals. The Scripture says, "If we confess our sins, He is faithful and righteous to forgive us our sins and to cleanse us from all unrighteousness" (1 John 1:9).

How can we keep sin's marks from becoming irreparable scars? Three simple tips will help. First, we must keep short accounts with God. When the Spirit of God convicts our hearts and minds of sin and we realize that something is wrong—something we thought, said, or did is offensive or displeasing to God—we should confess that sin immediately.

Second, we must seek God's forgiveness and cleansing. Forgiveness is necessary if the scars from sin are to be healed. Sometimes replanting is necessary, too. Repent, turn around, and fix it. We can't ignore it and assume that nobody will notice. We may be able to walk away from it and pretend nothing ever happened, but others who come along behind us (such as our marriage partner, children, and friends) will be impacted by the marks left by our lives. Let's give them a straight line to follow rather than an ugly, pockmarked, misleading line.

Third, we must own up to our responsibility, make right what was wrong as much as possible. If this involves restitution —going to someone and restoring what we have broken, stolen, or destroyed—then we must do this insofar as we are able. Sure that takes time, but not nearly as much as we may think. And the results are forgiveness, cleansing, healing, and restoration.

PRAYER

*Lord, please help me to recognize the marks
I have made and deal with them in a manner that
brings healing and restoration to others as well as myself.*

FURTHER READING
Psalm 32:1–6

HOW MUCH MUD?

Blessed are the pure in heart, for they shall see God.
MATTHEW 5:8

It doesn't take much mud on our ball to change the flight path of our shot. Unfortunately, the rules of golf prohibit us from wiping the ball clean while it is still in play during the approach to the green.

Similarly, it doesn't take much sin in our lives to throw us off course. And try as we might, sin won't come off without some divine help. We can scrub all we want, but our efforts will be to no avail.

Dr. Helen Roseveare, a medical missionary to Africa, related in her book *Living Holiness* a poignant story of Jaki, one of the one hundred orphan children for whom she and other missionaries were caring at a mission compound in Kenya. It was lunchtime and the children were happily splashing their hands in the cool water pool, washing off the dirt and grime, excitedly anticipating their delicious meal.

After they had paused to thank the Lord for the lunch, the children began pressing forward toward the food line, but not before they passed inspection. Each child had to show that his or her hands were clean before being permitted to go through the line.

On this day, Jaki had not paid close enough attention to the cleansing process that was supposed to have taken place at the pool. As he hurriedly attempted to sneak through inspection, the voice of authority was heard to say, "Jaki, go and wash your hands!"

"But, Miss, I have washed them!"

"Jaki, look at them—they're filthy!"

"Please, Miss, I did wash them! I did, I truly did."

"Jaki, just look at your hands. Are they clean?"

"But I washed—I washed. I really washed!" wailed the culprit. As Jaki turned to leave the line and make his way back to the water hole, the luckless lad could be heard muttering, "But how clean do my hands have to be to be clean?"[8]

Jaki's question hits the nail right on the head for most of

us. How clean is clean? Better still, how clean do I have to be to be pleasing in God's sight?

The psalmist pondered:

> Who may ascend into the hill of the LORD?
> And who may stand in His holy place?
> He who has clean hands and a pure heart,
> Who has not lifted up his soul to falsehood,
> And has not sworn deceitfully.
>
> PSALM 24:3–4

Who is going to see God? In the Beatitudes, Jesus said, "Blessed are the pure in heart, for they shall see God" (Matthew 5:8).

Pure in heart? Jesus, are You kidding? In a world filled with moral filth and ethical degradation, who talks about purity? In a world where cheaters usually win, who talks about purity? In a world where might makes right, and where nice guys finish last according to Leo Durocher, where *Nice Guys Sleep Alone* according to Bruce Feirstein, where nice guys finish their rounds in the dark according to Henry Beard in *Mulligan's Laws*—in such a world as ours, who talks about purity?

God does.

His standards do not vacillate with every whim of our

society. His commands remain the same. He requires that we be morally clean, pure, and spotless.

That creates a serious problem: Most of us are painfully aware of our failures and our sins, and we know that if forced to stand alone on our own merit before God, we wouldn't stand a chance of entering heaven.

God says we are to be holy, but we are not holy. We know that it is absolutely impossible to ever become holy by our own efforts. Just when we think our hands are clean and our heart is pure, God shines His searchlight on us and discloses the dirt that we allowed to remain hidden in the shadows of our lives.

The apostle Paul must have experienced something similar. See if you can identify with his sentiments:

> For that which I am doing, I do not understand; for I am not practicing what I would like to do, but I am doing the very thing I hate. . . . For the wishing is present in me, but the doing of the good is not. For the good that I wish, I do not do; but I practice the very evil that I do not wish. But if I am doing the very thing I do not wish, I am no longer the one doing it, but sin which dwells in me.
>
> ROMANS 7:15, 18–20

Paul saw the issues with stark clarity. He made no attempt to justify himself.

A little boy was constantly getting into trouble. Everywhere he went, trouble seemed to follow him. His Sunday school teacher, however, was a paragon of virtue, and the boy admired her immensely. One day as he was comparing his conduct to hers, he lamented with despair evident in his voice, "Teacher, you're so good, and I'm so bad. I just wish you could crawl down inside of me; then, I'd be good like you are!"

Though the youngster's theology leaves much to be desired, he unwittingly struck upon the secret to holiness. The key to Christlike conduct is "Christ in you, the hope of glory" (Colossians 1:27). Nowhere does the Word of God imply that successful Christian living depends upon our abilities, spiritual or otherwise. The Christian life doesn't involve us attempting to live up to God's standards. It relies on Him.

We can't measure up to God's standards. We cannot take away a single sin that we've committed. But thank God, Jesus can!

Do you remember Paul's pointed question after his despondent description of his defeat in the face of sin? Paul cried out, "Who will set me free from the body of this death?" Then he suddenly perceived the answer to his question: "Thanks be to God through Jesus Christ our Lord!" (Romans 7:24–25). Paul saw that Jesus was his only hope of holiness.

Christ's sacrifice on the cross purchased both our salvation from sin and the ability to live victoriously over sin. His blood paid the total price for our full salvation.

The stain of sin can be cleansed only when we ask God to forgive us. He washes us thoroughly from the inside out. Here's some really good news: Once we have been cleansed by God, He gives us the power to fly straight.

PRAYER
It seems I have an uncanny knack
for allowing dirt to cover my soul.
I know that my strongest detergents are insufficient
to cleanse the stains caused by sin.
But thank You, Lord, that Your blood cleanses completely
and Your power is more than enough to set me free.

FURTHER READING
Psalm 51

HOME ON THE RANGE

Go into all the world and preach
the gospel to all creation.
MARK 16:15.

Why is it that most golfers can go to the driving range and blast one shot after another 200 yards, 250 yards, 300 yards, and sometimes even farther, but when they get on the golf course and tee it up at number one, it's as though they left all those great shots home on the range? We all know that if we could retrieve some of those fabulous driving range whoppers, we might be able to bring our score down a dozen strokes.

Several explanations for those phenomenal driving range escapades should be considered. First, the accuracy of driving range yardage markers is about as reliable as your least favorite politician's latest campaign promises. Most range markers seem to have been measured by a guy named Zaccheus, and tend to be about 10 to 15 percent off, on the high side. In other words, the 250-yard marker may in fact be only about 200 yards away.

"Why would the range owners do such a thing?" you might ask. Easy. The driving range is more fun for the customers if they think they are really pounding drives to infinity and beyond. Who wants to go home from the range knowing that they only hit the ball a measly 125 yards?

Another factor that increases distance at a driving range is the hardness of the "fairways." At most good golf courses, the fairways are watered and cut daily and even in dry weather will allow the ball to roll only twenty or thirty yards. On the other hand, bouncing a ball off most driving range fairways is like bouncing it off the cart path. The hard, dry grass will often let a ball roll four times as far as the same shot might roll on a real fairway.

Furthermore, because of the enormous number of balls struck from them, many driving ranges use flat, smooth, "welcome mat" tee boxes with a bit of rubber tubing stuck in them as a tee. That is an entirely different feel than teeing up on manicured grass. Hitting balls off the welcome mat is not the same as hitting them on the course. Maybe that's why when we take the same swing out to the first tee box, people in the clubhouse head for cover.

Jesus never intended for us to stay at "home on the range," to live our Christian lives on the practice tee. He wants us to get out there in the real world and to begin having an influence. Many of us are too content to spend our lives in comfortable circumstances, often surrounded by fellow believers who tend to tell us that we are hitting 250-yard drives inside the church sanctuary, when in reality, we are grossly overestimating our effectiveness. It's time to get on the course where the real game is played.

At the close of His ministry on earth, Jesus issued a firm command to His disciples: "All authority has been given to Me in heaven and on earth. Go therefore and make disciples of all the nations, baptizing them in the name of the Father and the Son and the Holy Spirit, teaching them to observe all that I commanded you; and lo, I am with you always, even to the end of the age" (Matthew 28:18–20).

This command is commonly referred to as the Great Commission because it is one of the Lord's last bits of instruction to His disciples before He ascended back into heaven. It is a clarion call to evangelize the world. If our efforts in spreading the good news fall short of this command, we are failing to follow through on one of the key assignments Jesus has given to us.

But notice, it is not enough to evangelize. Jesus has called us to make disciples, to help new believers become strong, lasting disciples, not merely new converts. Our going, baptizing, and teaching have the singular purpose of making disciples. That is the real game. And it cannot be played while staying home on the range.

PRAYER
Lord, as much as I appreciate my practice time,
I want to get into the real game.
Send me out with Your power and Your presence
to be a representative of You to the world.

FURTHER READING
Isaiah 6:1–8

MONEY MATTERS

From everyone who has been given
much shall much be required.
LUKE 12:48

LPGA pro Barb Thomas was intrigued when her pastor challenged the congregation in a very tangible way to be good stewards of what God had given them. The church, Scottsdale Bible Church in Arizona, handed out 2,400 ten-dollar bills to members of the congregation with the instructions that they were to multiply this money over the next three months to help raise money for a missions project in India.

After Pastor Darryl Delhousaye preached a sermon on Luke 19, the parable of the talents, the money was distributed.

As the money was passed out, the pastor told the congregation, "You know for certain that the ten dollars you hold in your hand is not your money. It is God's money. You didn't earn it—it was given to you by God. That money is 'seed' money. In the next three months, take this seed—take God's money—and steward it. That is, increase it."

Barb Thomas decided that she would use God's ten dollars that had been placed in her hands as part of her entry fee into her next LPGA tournament, the Hawaiian Ladies Open in Honolulu. She committed to herself and to the Lord that she would give 10 percent of whatever money she made by competing in the tournament to the missions project.

The first two days of the tournament, Barb fired rounds of 68 and 66 and found herself perched atop the leader board. In the pressroom after the second round, Barb confided, "I'd like to share a story with you, but one thing I'd like you to know is that I don't think I have some special 'in' with God and that He's pulling for me and nobody else. I do believe the Lord has given me a peace on the course that allows me to play to the best of my ability and to use the talents He's given me."

Then she went on and told the press about how she had used God's ten dollars to enter the tournament and that 10 percent of her earnings would go toward the India project, whether she won $2,000 or the top prize of $82,000.

During the final round of the tournament, Barb prayed, "Lord, this thing is in Your hands. Whatever You want to do with it, it's in Your hands. I accept whatever You have planned for me in this tournament, because You know the need."

With that thought in mind, Barb went on to win the tournament, her first victory after twelve years of being on the Tour.

Barb was interviewed over the public address system while still on the eighteenth green so the gallery could share in the victory celebration. With hundreds of people listening in the crowd and potentially millions more observing the interview through the media, a reporter asked Barb to tell the story about the church mission project and the ten-dollar bill that had been part of her entry fee.

Barb gladly recounted the events surrounding her commitment of 10 percent of her winnings to the India missions project, and when she concluded the story, the audience burst into applause.

A few weeks later, a reporter asked Barb about giving away the first 10 percent of her $82,000 prize money. "Were you ever tempted to give, say, only $2,000?" the reporter queried.

"That never crossed my mind," Barb replied matter-of-factly.[9]

While we may never win a golf tournament or be in a position to give away such a large amount of money, the most important issue is not the amount we have to give. It is being faithful in being a good steward of whatever God gives us.

PRAYER

My financial gifts are merely a token of
my dependence on You, O Lord.
As I give back to You from the money
You entrust to my care,
I am reminded that You own all that I have
and that I am managing Your resources for You.

FURTHER READING
Luke 19:12–27; Luke 6:38

WHEN WORDS CAN'T
SAY ENOUGH

Let the words of my mouth and
the meditation of my heart
be acceptable in Thy sight, O LORD,
my rock and my Redeemer.
PSALM 19:14

Many people have trouble expressing their innermost thoughts and feelings. As one country crooner put it, "I'm not much good at love out loud." For many of us, this is especially true when we are trying to express our faith in the Lord.

But take heart. We don't have to be a great public speaker

to be a positive witness for the Lord.

At the 1995 B.C. Open in Endicott, New York, Johnny Hart, the cartoonist who draws the comic strip for whom the tournament is named, hosted a prayer breakfast. Before PGA Tour player David Ogrin delivered the keynote message, Hart was asked to give "a short testimony." The five-foot, seven-inch cartoonist responded, "I am a short testimony!" Hart then stood up and gave a brief word of encouragement. "Jesus Christ is Lord," he declared enthusiastically, and then sat down.[10]

In the Bible, we find another short testimony of Christ's power to change lives. The man Zaccheus was not only a tax collector—a despised occupation among Jews since most tax collectors of that time were in collusion with the oppressive Roman Empire—he was a chief tax collector. To modernize the story, think of Zaccheus as a little guy who was a big shot with the Internal Revenue Service. The government for whom Zaccheus worked, however, was not his own. The money he collected did not go toward improving the quality of life of the people of Israel. Zaccheus collected money from the Jewish people to help finance Roman excess.

Apparently, Zaccheus was good at his job, because the Scripture points out that he was a rich man (Luke 19:2). Part of Zaccheus's wealth came from money he skimmed off the taxes he collected. He wouldn't dare cheat the Romans, but to overcharge his own people. . .well, that was a different matter.

Zaccheus was in the crowd on the day Jesus passed through Jericho on His way to Jerusalem. Zaccheus had heard rumors about Jesus, and this was his opportunity to see the man for himself.

But Zaccheus had one problem—his size. He was short, real short. Try as he might, he could not see Jesus above the heads of the people around him. It doesn't take much effort to assume that the Jewish citizens from whom Zaccheus had alienated himself made little effort to open a spot through which the tax collector could peek. In desperation (and exasperation?), Zaccheus ran ahead of the masses and scurried up a sycamore tree so he could get an unobstructed glimpse of Jesus.

What a shock it must have been to that crowd when Jesus spied the runt and called out to him, "Zaccheus, hurry and come down, for today I must stay at your house" (Luke 19:5).

Zaccheus clambered down out of his perch. One of the first things he said to Jesus was, "Behold, Lord, half of my possessions I will give to the poor, and if I have defrauded anyone of anything, I will give back four times as much" (v. 8).

Notice how Zaccheus understated the situation when he declared, "If I have defrauded anyone"? The Jewish people had no doubts about how much they had been cheated. Like Zaccheus, none of us wants to admit the full extent of our sins.

But if Zaccheus was conservative in estimating the damage he had done, he was just as generous when trying to make things right. He offered to repay four times the amount taken—far more than the law demanded of a cheat who had been caught.

Apparently, Jesus was pleased with the transformation that had taken place in Zaccheus's heart, for the Lord said, "Today salvation has come to this house, because he, too, is a son of Abraham" (v. 9). Jesus went on to explain, "For the Son of Man has come to seek and to save that which was lost" (v. 10).

We don't have to get our words just right. Sometimes, the best short testimony we can give is the testimony of God's amazing grace: "I once was lost, but now I'm found; was blind but now I see."

PRAYER

Father, may my life be so filled with You that
I do not have to open my mouth to let people know
that I am a follower of Jesus Christ.
Let me not only witness about You,
but let me be a witness of You.

FURTHER READING
Acts 1:1–8

CONQUERING
HANDICAPS

We do not lose heart.
2 CORINTHIANS 4:1

The case of Casey Martin versus the PGA dominated many golf discussions during the 1997–98 golf season. Because of a disability which made it difficult for the young golfer to walk the course, Martin sued for, and won, the right to ride in a golf cart while he competed in PGA events. But Casey Martin was by no means the first fellow to overcome a handicap on the links.

The legendary Tommy Armour lost an eye in World

War I, but he overcame the disability and became a PGA champion. Armour won the U.S. Open in 1927, the first of three major titles the one-eyed pro would capture. In 1930, Armour won the PGA Championship, and the following year, he took the cup at the British Open.

Charles Boswell of Birmingham, Alabama, is another golfer who proved that nothing could keep him away from the game he loved. Although he never played professionally and never won an amateur tournament of any kind, Charles Boswell did shoot an amazing round of 81 one time.

What's so amazing about shooting 81? Charles Boswell was blind. Furthermore, he had never played golf before he was blinded by shell fire during World War II. Just goes to show that we really can overcome our handicaps if we don't give up.

Some people never quite make it in life because they give up too easily. They have all the reasons (or excuses) for why they should quit:

- I don't have enough education.
- My wife (or husband) and I can't get along.
- I'm too old.
- I'm too young.
- I have a physical disability.

- I don't have enough money.
- I'm from the wrong side of the tracks.
- I'm codependent.
- I'm a child of an alcoholic (or a drug addict, or a person with some other compulsion).
- I was abused as a child.

Many of these statements are valid. Nevertheless, most of the world's "Horatio Alger" stories belong not to the extremely talented, but to the extremely persistent. Nearly all of them experienced serious failure or misfortune at some point in their lives.

What we don't have or can't do doesn't matter. What really counts is what we do with what God has given us. The writer to the Hebrews put it this way:

> Therefore, since we have so great a cloud of witnesses surrounding us, let us also lay aside every encumbrance, and the sin which so easily entangles us, and let us run with endurance the race that is set before us, fixing our eyes on Jesus, the author and perfecter of faith, who for the joy set before Him endured the cross, despising the shame, and

has sat down at the right hand of the throne of God. For consider Him who has endured such hostility by sinners against Himself, so that you may not grow weary and lose heart.

HEBREWS 12:1–3

PRAYER

Rather than focusing on my handicaps,
those capabilities that I do not have, Father,
help me to concentrate on all the good things I have,
the many blessings that You have
so freely poured into my life,
the many things I can do to
bring honor to Your great name.

FURTHER READING
2 Corinthians 4:8–10

A NEW BEGINNING

Forgetting what lies behind and reaching forward
to what lies ahead,
I press on toward the goal for the prize
of the upward call of God in Christ Jesus.
PHILIPPIANS 3:13–14

Few golf fans will ever forget the incredible finish to the 1995 British Open in which Italian superstar Costantino Rocca was chasing the leader, John Daly. Rocca was behind by two shots when he blew a relatively easy chip shot, leaving his ball short of the green on the eighteenth hole. Even the most sedate fans crowded around the green gasped in horror as they watched Rocca's shot fall thirty feet short.

It's all over, everyone thought—everyone that is, except Costantino Rocca. He faced a nearly impossible shot, but you would not have guessed it by looking at him. Rocca took a deep breath, stepped up to his ball, and knocked a thirty-footer directly into the hole, tying the match and sending the Open into a play-off.

Everyone hits a bad shot once in a while. We can dwell on it and allow it to destroy our concentration and future shots, or we can let it go, start fresh with the next stroke or hole, and do things correctly. The choice is ours.

Good golfers learn how to recover after a lousy shot (round, tournament, or year!). Sure, when they review their play they recall their error, but in the heat of competition, they know that they must win the battle of the mind and heart; they must keep pressing on.

Every new day offers a perfect opportunity to start fresh. Maybe there are some areas of our lives that cry out for more attention. Okay, so we've blown it in a few areas. Maybe we have been doing some things that we know are causing us to lose out with our family, friends, or with God. Whatever the case, now is the time to settle the past and move on.

We should fix what we can—apologize, repent, and do our best to restore fractured relationships—then forget those things that are behind us. They are done. We cannot change them. Let's look forward to the good things that God has in store for us as we concentrate on Him. The next shot is up to us. Let it be the start of a brand-new game.

PRAYER

It is no great surprise to You, Lord,
to know that I've blown more
than my share of shots in this life.
But it is surprising to me to discover just how much
You want to help me recover and start fresh.
Thank You, Father,
for a new beginning!

FURTHER READING

2 Corinthians 5

THE
REAL THING

*For they themselves report about us
what kind of a reception we had with you,
and how you turned to God from idols
to serve a living and true God,
and to wait for His Son from heaven,
whom He raised from the dead,
that is Jesus,
who delivers us from
the wrath to come.*
1 THESSALONIANS 1:9–10

Let's face it: It's easy for us to lose our Christian testimony on a golf course. Sometimes we say or do some seemingly insignificant thing, but it may leave an indelibly negative impression. "Hmph," some onlooker grunts, "I thought they were supposed to be Christians!"

The apostle Paul lists at least three marks of a true Christian in 1 Thessalonians 1:9–10. Paul was writing to a group of new believers in Thessalonica, a town famous for its pagan idol worship. Paul had only been able to instruct these new believers in person for three weeks before he had been forced to flee for his life. You can imagine how elated the apostle was when word came to him that the Thessalonians' conversion had been thoroughly genuine and that despite persecutions, they were staying committed to the Lord.

Three evidences convinced Paul that the Thessalonians were for real: 1) They had turned to God and from their idols; 2) They were now serving the living and true God; and 3) They were waiting for the return of Jesus Christ.

These new Christians immediately realized that they couldn't cling to both Jesus and their idols. To wholeheartedly serve God, they first had to do some housecleaning, which included getting rid of their idols.

When we think of idols, we tend to conjure up images of primitive religious practices among native people. But many idol worshipers wear designer clothing, play golf at great courses, and work in brightly lit offices.

What is an idol? Anything that stands between us and God and takes the place that rightfully belongs to Jesus Christ in our life becomes an idol for us. It could be a good gift from God that we have allowed to take precedence over Him. It may be our job, our spouse or other family members, our car, our athletic or intellectual capabilities, our physical appearance, or even our refrigerator (think about that one!). On the other hand, we may have allowed something destructive to become an idol. We could be worshiping the idol of drugs, alcohol, or tobacco. Maybe we are bowing to an idol created by an attitude of lust, greed, or pride.

Whether our idol is a "good" thing or a "bad" thing is irrelevant. If we are worshiping an idol, we are not worshiping Jesus. One of the basic commandments is: "You shall have no other gods before Me. You shall not make for yourself an idol, or any likeness of what is in heaven above or on the earth beneath or in the water under the earth. You shall not worship them or serve them; for I, the LORD your God, am a jealous God" (Exodus 20:3–5).

Not only did the Thessalonians turn from their lifeless wooden and stone idols, but they also began to serve the living and true God. Sometimes, we may wonder why

God wants somebody like us to serve Him. At a snap of His supernatural fingers, He could have ten thousand angels ready to do His will. And they wouldn't give Him any back talk either! Why does God want us to serve Him?

It's not that complicated, really. We serve the living and true God as an expression of our love to Him. That's it. Jesus said, "You are My friends, if you do what I command you" (John 15:14). He doesn't want us to serve Him out of fear that He is going to zap us with lightning if we don't. He knows that we show our love for Him by how we live for Him.

An amazing by-product of service is joy. Jesus spelled it out this way: "If you keep My commandments, you will abide in My love; just as I have kept My Father's commandments, and abide in His love. These things I have spoken to you, that My joy may be in you, and that your joy may be made full" (John 15:10–11).

If our main goal in life is something other than loving and serving God, we will experience constant tension and turmoil. We were made to love and serve the living and true God. When we do, we find joy, happiness, peace, and a sense of meaning that comes from knowing that we are doing what we were created to do. Each day becomes an exciting adventure, filled with new opportunities to serve Him until He

comes! Do something today that has positive eternal consequences. Simply put, do something you know will make Jesus
happy. You'll be happy you did.

PRAYER
May my Christian life be one that bears evidence
that I am a true believer, not just
when everything is going well,
but in difficult times as well.

FURTHER READING
1 Thessalonians 1:1–10

KEEP
YOUR EYE
ON THE BALL

O you of little faith,
why did you doubt?
MATTHEW 14:31

A generally accepted theory about hitting a golf ball is that you must be able to see it when you swing at it. Although this theory has been proven incorrect by innumerable duffers and even a few professionals, it is still widely held to be true among most golf teachers. The idea is that if you don't allow your head to move too much during your swing, you have a much better chance of striking the ball squarely.

If you move your head along the path of your backswing, your body will sway to the right and you won't be able to keep your weight directly over the ball, a necessary evil if you want your body to pivot correctly. On the other hand, if you keep your head relatively still, concentrating on the ball as you swing, your body pivots around an imaginary pole that runs from the top of your head to a point on the ground between your feet. This helps bring your right shoulder around just below your chin as you make square contact with the ball.

If you take your eye off the ball even for a fraction of a second as you swing through, however, you are tempted to sway to the left on your downswing, which is a surefire way to produce a lousy shot. Although many pros and pundits discount the advice, for most of us, keeping your eye on the ball is essential.

The reason some of us have such difficulty keeping our head down and our eyes on the ball is a lack of faith. We are not really confident that we are going to hit the ball where we want it to go. So we find ourselves tempted to take an ever-so-slight peek at the fairway as we swing, just to make sure that we can find our ball after we hit it.

Lack of confidence can ruin us on the golf course. If we aren't confident, we can't get our muscles to relax; we can't believe that we can do what needs to be done. We start thinking, *Oh, boy, I really have to swing for the moon on this shot because I'm not sure I have enough club to make it.* Typically such lack of confidence causes us to lose our concentration. We take our eyes off the ball, our head jerks up as we swing, and we quickly discover that all our fears were well founded. The one thing that is not so easily found is our ball.

The apostle Peter knew something about why concentration and confidence went together. One night, somewhere between 3:00 and 6:00 A.M., Peter and his fellow disciples were enduring some rough weather on the Sea of Galilee. Suddenly the fishermen-turned-preachers saw something that looked like a ghost coming toward them on the water. The tough, strong, experienced seamen cried out in fear.

Then Jesus called out to them, "Take courage. It is I; do not be afraid." Amazingly, He was walking on the water in their direction.

Peter said, "Lord, if it's really you, let me walk out to you on the water."

And Jesus said, "Come!"

Peter started out well. He stepped out of the boat. That's incredible in itself if you think about it. This experienced fisherman stepped out of the boat without a life jacket, rope, or anything else to hold him up. But with his confidence in Jesus, Peter put one foot, then the other into the water. And for a time, the fisherman defied all the principles of nature. Peter walked on water!

But when he took his eyes off Jesus, he noticed the wind and the waves, and he became afraid. That's when Peter took an unexpected plunge.

No doubt, the other disciples were back in the boat, laughing and making fun. "Hey, Pete, you lifted up your head. You took your eyes off the ball. You dummy. What made you ever think that you could pull off a shot like that?"

For his part, Peter at least had the good sense to know where to place his confidence. He immediately called out to Jesus, "Lord, save me!"

And Jesus did. He reached out His hand and pulled Peter to safety. Apparently Peter was only an arm's length away from Jesus, and yet his faith was shaken by circumstances (Matthew 14:25–31).

At times, all of us have our faith severely tested by life's circumstances, even those of us who are trying with all our hearts, minds, and souls to walk with the Lord. When those testings come, keep your eyes on Jesus; try not to let the whirling wind and the roaring waves overwhelm you.

Keep trusting Him. If you fall, call out to Jesus; He will be there, just an arm's length away, to pick you up and draw you to safety.

PRAYER
Lord, let my faith increase,
teach me to trust You more fully.
It's relatively easy to trust You
for those things I can see,
but when the darkness moves in,
or the wind and waves assail,
I want You to know that I still believe in You.

FURTHER READING
Matthew 14:22–33

BEAUTY AND THE BEST

The fool has said in his heart, "There is no God."
PSALM 14:1

One of the great joys of playing golf is that you get to see some of the most beautiful landscapes in the world. The truly spectacular golf courses are almost always built near some natural wonder, and for good reason. Would Pebble Beach with its fabulous view of the Pacific, for instance, be the majestic course it is if it were set in Chicago?

With all due respect to the great golf course designers who have built modern, man-made wonders, the original course designer is God. Our best efforts to create fabulous, lush environments are a pale reproduction of something He thought up a long time ago. Only a fool would fail to see God's hand in creation; only a fool would say there is no God.

The apostle Paul makes a strong point when he says that nature itself bears witness of God's existence. Paul wrote to the Romans:

> For the wrath of God is revealed from heaven against all ungodliness and unrighteousness of men, who suppress the truth in unrighteousness, because that which is known about God is evident within them; for God made it evident to them. For since the creation of the world His invisible attributes, His eternal power and divine nature, have been clearly seen, being understood through what has been made, so that they are without excuse. For even though they knew God, they did not honor Him as God, or give thanks; but they became futile in their speculations, and their foolish heart was darkened. Professing to be wise, they became fools.
>
> ROMANS 1:18–22

The apostle was confronting the lie that asks, "How can God hold me accountable for my actions? I don't even know if He exists!" Paul replied that simply by looking at the world around us, we should be able to see enough evidence of God's existence to put our faith and trust in Him.

When we choose to believe in God, the world suddenly takes on a whole new appearance. Next time you are striding up a fairway—or even looking in the woods for a lost ball—stop for a moment. Look around at the natural beauty of God's creation. Few things on earth are more pleasing to the eye than a gorgeous golf course. Notice the trees, the flowers, the green grass, the streams or ponds, canyons or hillsides, and yes, even the sand, each grain individually and uniquely created by our loving heavenly Father. Allow the scene to cause praise and adoration of the Lord to well within you. This is your Father's world.

The evidence for God's existence is in—actually it's been in since the creation of the world. Only a fool would ignore it. . . and you are no fool.

PRAYER
In my haste to get where I want to go,
help me, Lord,
to notice Your handiwork all around me.
Let Your creation bring praise to Your great name.

FURTHER READING
Romans 1:1–21

AVOIDING
CALLOUSES

But encourage one another day after day,
as long as it is still called "Today,"
lest any one of you be hardened
by the deceitfulness of sin.
HEBREWS 3:13

Some calluses on our hands are good for our game, especially those that come from hours of practice on the range. Most calluses, however, are indicators that something is wrong with our grip or swing. We may be holding the club too tightly, causing our muscles to become too tense, which inevitably leads to poor shots. If we are gripping the club tightly enough to produce calluses, we are probably also getting used to seeing our two-dollar balls produce ugly splashes in golf course ponds and cutting newfound paths through the boonies. And then there's the small detail of what that grip does to our golf glove and the grips on our clubs.

The renowned golf coach John Redman once challenged Muffin Spencer-Devlin about her strong grip. "You're gripping the club too tightly," Redman scolded the LPGA pro. He instructed Muffin to hold the club more naturally, with her left hand on the club just the way it hung by her side when she was relaxed. It was a watershed day in Spencer-Devlin's game when she learned to loosen her grip.

Other kinds of calluses can be equally destructive. For instance, Steve Green is the possessor of a rare, golden treasure —his voice. Few vocalists can sing with such lilting intensity, such clarity, and such sheer power. The secret to his unusual ability lies in two tiny vocal cords at the base of his throat.

Within months after receiving Christian music's "Male Vocalist of the Year" Award, Steve had an anxious appointment with a doctor who specializes in vocal cord examinations. The singer described the doctor's delicate procedure: "He put a probe with a camera on the end of it up through my nasal cavity and down into my throat. Then he asked me to sing! And the song he wanted me to sing was 'A Mighty Fortress is Our God' [the Martin Luther classic that Steve belts out in an unparalleled a capella rendition]. While I was singing, the doctor videotaped my vocal cords as they vibrated against each other." Steve paused and whimsically commented, "And for those of you who are interested, we'll have tapes available in the lobby after the concert."

Why would anyone submit to such an ordeal?

"Because," said Steve, "there is always the danger that small, barely perceptible calluses can develop on your vocal cords if you are not careful. You can't see them, you can't feel them, and they don't really affect your voice. They are called pre-nodes."[11]

These pre-nodes, if undetected, can develop into full-fledged nodules on a person's vocal cords, which must be removed. The nodules, or their removal, can greatly alter and sometimes even destroy a person's vocal ability. As a result, some individuals talk or sing with a heavy raspiness for the rest of their lives. Certainly, a few singers have parleyed these raspy sounds into hit records and extremely successful music careers. Kenny Rogers, Phil Driscoll, Kim Carnes, and Joe Cocker are prime examples. But for a crisp, clear singer such as Steve Green, vocal cord nodules would be a disaster.

The most dangerous aspect of pre-nodes, remember, is their subtlety; you don't notice them until it is too late. The destructive calluses have already formed. The writer to the Hebrews warned us to beware that we don't allow the cords of our heart to become callused. His prescription for a preventive examination doesn't include a videotape, but it is pretty revealing: "Take care, brethren, lest there should be in any one of you an evil, unbelieving heart, in falling away from the living God. But encourage one another day after day, as long as it is still called, 'Today,' lest any one of you be hardened by the deceitfulness of sin" (Hebrews 3:12–13).

How do our hearts grow callused? One certain way of becoming hardened and insensitive, says the writer to the Hebrews, is through the deceitfulness of sin (v. 13). That word *deceitfulness* could be translated glamour; we can become blinded by the glamour of sin.

Have you ever noticed that Satan makes sin look mighty enticing? He shows us the comedic beer commercials on TV and gets us laughing about conversations or conduct that go against what we know is right. Or he shows us magazines filled with photos of the beautiful people as they supposedly live life to the hilt. What the devil does not show us is the people who thought they could drink and drive and whose brains are splattered all over the dashboard after slamming into a tree on their way home from the party.

The devil attempts to titillate our senses with pictures of a naked, unmarried couple wrapped in a passionate embrace. What the deceiver does not show us is the guilt and shame of immorality, the pain of a broken marriage, or the horrors of being infected by AIDS or other sexually transmitted diseases.

Of course sin is attractive at first glance. If sin wasn't fun, nobody would do it! But remember the devil is a liar, and he's out to steal, kill, and destroy you. Don't allow the devil to deceive you. Don't allow slight improprieties to cause your heart to become callous, insensitive, and unresponsive to the Spirit of the Lord.

What is the cure for this sort of callousness? The writer of Hebrews said, "Encourage one another day after day" (v. 13). We are to encourage each other, not just once in awhile, but daily! The word encourage means "to support, to lift up, to strengthen," and that is what God calls each of us to do. You may not be able to hit a golf ball like Muffin Spencer-Devlin or sing like Steve Green, but you can use your God-given abilities to be an encouragement to someone else.

Make it a habit to encourage someone every day. You may keep someone from becoming hard-hearted; you may prevent someone from becoming insensitive and calloused; and that someone might just be you!

PRAYER
Lord, it takes so little time and effort
to offer a word of encouragement.
Help me to be sensitive to
the opportunities before me.
Keep my heart clear of calluses
that would hinder me
from sensing Your heart.

FURTHER READING
Hebrews 3:7–4:2

A MATTER OF
TASTE

For the kingdom of God
is not eating and drinking,
but righteousness and peace and joy
in the Holy Spirit.
ROMANS 14:17

There is no accounting for some people's tastes, even on the golf course. Some are traditionalists, while others like to push the envelope. Still others simply enjoy doing their own thing and couldn't care less what anyone else thinks or says about them.

Take clothing for example: Where once the most outlandish golf course apparel was a pair of checkered pants, today pro golfers such as Doug Sanders can be seen wearing outfits that rival NFL uniforms, including the golf shoes he has dyed to match his clothing. Similarly, Jasper Parnevik is known for his upturned visor, his choice of colorful pants, and wide-collared, zippered shirts. And Payne Stewart wears knickers on the Tour. It's all a matter of taste.

Golf clothing aside, a wide diversity of opinion exists concerning the golf swing itself. Miller Barber's swing was often described as catching the club in a clothesline. His unorthodox swing allowed his right elbow to stick out on the backswing—something every golf pro says is a kiss of death. Unless you are Miller Barber, that is. Miller was a consistent winner on the PGA Tour during the 1960s and '70s, and he won twenty-four times during the first nine years the Senior PGA Tour was in operation.

More recently, Jim Furyk, another player with an unusual swing, has done okay for himself, much to the consternation of golf teachers everywhere. Furyk's name regularly lands high on the leader board, and at one point in 1997 he had eight straight top-ten finishes. On the other hand, Ernie Els has a classic, smooth, fluid swing that produces consistently accurate shots. Since 1994, the six-foot, three-inch South

African star has won at least one PGA event each year, including two U.S. Opens.

Clearly after one has learned the basics of the game, much of golf is a matter of personal convictions. What feels right and works for you on a consistent basis is what really matters.

Not surprisingly, both on and off the golf course, even devout Christians differ on their personal convictions and tastes, so don't go bananas when you find yourself eyeball to eyeball with someone who doesn't see things your way. Granted, biblical principles are to be obeyed scrupulously. "Thou shalt not" means thou shalt not, and "Thou shalt" means thou shalt.

Pretty simple so far, right? But when it comes to the realm of personal convictions, the number of distinctive nuances among Christians varies almost as much as golf swings. Music, foods and beverages, clothing styles, length and color of hair, and local taboos are just a few areas where the opinions of the saints run a wide gamut.

For instance, nothing tends to categorize current Christians more quickly than contemporary music. Some saints swoon at the soft, soothing sounds of Sandi Patty or Point of Grace or at the graceful harmonies of 4Him. Others enjoy the more raucous rock of the Newsboys or Jars of Clay. Still others have never heard of the above artists and are quite content to sing the old hymns of the church.

A similar variety can be found when it comes to clothing and hairstyles among Christians. The perennial problems between parents and teenagers will probably never change.

In Paul's day, the discussion wasn't over golf swings, music, or hairstyles. The controversy boiled around the issue: Should a dedicated follower of Jesus eat meat that was sacrificed to idols?

"Why not?" asked some well-meaning Christians. "We don't believe in those false gods. And it is the choicest meat available. Not only that, it is the best bargain in town." These believers were right, too. The heathen worshipers of pagan gods were required to sacrifice their finest animals, after which they were not permitted to touch a single slice of the meat. Consequently it was discount steak and burger time, and the early Christians had no qualms about scarfing up a good deal.

That is, some of them didn't. Other saints were appalled that their fellow believers could stoop so low as to eat meat that was consecrated to idols. It was contaminated, according to their tastes.

You can pick up Paul's opinion about this palatal problem in Romans 14. Notice carefully the balance between verses 17 and 23.

The apostle instructs us to "accept the one who is weak in faith" (14:1), but curiously, the weaker person to whom Paul refers is the one who is bound by legalism. We tend to view the issue from the opposite pole, regarding the person who attempts to follow a stringent set of nonessential regulations as the "stronger" brother or sister. "Not so," says Paul.

Nevertheless, we are to accept each other, in spite of our spiritual quirks and idiosyncracies for at least four reasons: 1) God has accepted our weaker brother or sister (v. 3). Therefore who are we to judge a person that our heavenly Father has accepted? 2) The Lord will cause our weaker brothers to stand (v. 4). We may think they are going to wipe out if they don't do everything exactly like we do, but God will hold them up. 3) Jesus is Lord of all those who truly believe in Him and are striving to obey His commands (vv. 6–9). Yes, even Lord of those who don't agree with us! 4) We will all be judged before God and will have to give an account for the way we have lived our lives (vv. 10–12).

As a further word of warning, Paul reminded us, "The faith which you have, have as your own conviction before God. Happy is he who does not condemn himself in what he approves" (Romans 14:22).

We don't have to agree with everyone else's convictions, but we must respect our brothers and sisters' right to hold those views and give them the space to work out the details of their own relationship with Jesus.

Paul summed it up by saying, "Therefore, let us not judge one another anymore, but rather determine this—not to put an obstacle or a stumbling block in a brother's way" (v. 13).

PRAYER
Lord, please help me to be tolerant of
those people whose ideas, personal convictions,
and lifestyles are not that of my own.
In all things, may I love others
unconditionally with the love of Jesus.

FURTHER READING
Romans 14

GIVING GOD A TIP

Bring the whole tithe into the storehouse,
so that there may be food in My house,
and test Me now in this, says the LORD of hosts,
if I will not open for you the windows of heaven
and pour out for you a blessing
until it overflows.
MALACHI 3:10

Most pros pay their caddies between 7 and 10 percent of their winnings. For example, during an eleven-month stretch in 1991–92, Fred Couples won $2.5 million, out of which he paid his caddie, Joe LaCava, a cool $200,000. If a golfer gives his caddie that much money for helping him navigate the Tour courses, how much more should we show our appreciation to the Lord for His blessings in our lives!

In the Old Testament, 10 percent was a standard tithe of one's income. That amount was to be given automatically to God. Offerings were any amounts given over the tithe. Interestingly the tithe is barely mentioned in the New Testament. It is not that God now expects less than 10 percent of our income. Quite the contrary, Jesus wants to be Lord of what we do with the remaining 90 percent as well as the first 10 percent. He wants to be Lord of all.

God does not want us to become enamored by materialism; He doesn't want us to be possessive, sticky-fingered, money-grabbers. But God does want to bless His people and take good care of us. The Lord has promised that He will provide for us. As we honor Him by using the resources that He gives us for His glory, He will continue to pour out even greater blessings upon us.

Speaking through the prophet Malachi, God challenges us to test His veracity in this area:

> "Will a man rob God? Yet you are robbing Me!
> But you say, 'How have we robbed Thee?' In
> tithes and offering. You are cursed with a curse,
> for you are robbing Me, the whole nation of you!

Bring the whole tithe into the storehouse, so that there may be food in My house, and test Me now in this," says the LORD of hosts, "if I will not open for you the windows of heaven, and pour out for you a blessing until it overflows. Then I will rebuke the devourer for you, so that it may not destroy the fruits of the ground; nor will your vine in the field cast its grapes," says the LORD of hosts.

MALACHI 3:8–11

Notice: Not only do we rob God if we refuse to give Him "the tithe," the first 10 percent of our resources—defined by many as not just our money, but our time, talents, and treasures—but when we refuse to give, we rob ourselves. The Lord invites us to prove Him, to test Him, to check Him out to see if His promise of blessing is true. Furthermore, He promises to "rebuke the devourer" for those who will put Him first in their finances. The devourer is the devil, who is trying to destroy the fruit of our labors, and God promises that as we trust Him, the devil will be turned back. Why should we foolishly try to stand against the enemy in our own strength when God has promised that we can depend on Him?

Yet many Christians do just that, and they end up getting devoured by debt, which often leads to their being devoured by the devil in many other areas of their lives, as well. If you are not presently giving a tithe of your time, talents, and treasure to God, begin to do so. But don't stop there. The tithe is a minimum requirement, not a maximum goal.

PRAYER
Lord, no other area so starkly exposes
my true priorities as that of my finances.
In my checkbook and bank statements,
I can see quite clearly what really matters to me.
Please give me a heart and mind-set
that aligns my financial statements with those things
that You deem most important.

FURTHER READING
2 Corinthians 9:6–15

DEATH,
WHERE IS YOUR STING?

But I would not have you to be ignorant, brethren,
concerning them which are asleep,
that ye sorrow not,
even as others which have no hope.
1 THESSALONIANS 4:13 KJV

When Stuart Appleby chipped in for birdie from forty feet on the eighteenth hole at the 1998 PGA Championship, the crowd roared its approval. Appleby raised his putter in appreciation for the applause. Appleby hadn't won the PGA; he didn't even make the cut. But to the fans at Sahalee Country

Club outside Redmond, Washington, Appleby was a clear winner. No, he hadn't beaten the field of golfers; he had beaten something much more ominous.

Less than a month earlier, Stuart's wife, Renay, had been crushed to death between two cars at a London train station. Still grieving her loss, Appleby decided he had to get back to work and entered the PGA tournament, his first since Renay's death. Although Appleby shot a less-than-stellar 150 over the first two days of the tournament, the fans did not care. They cheered enthusiastically even when the twenty-seven-year-old widower sunk bogey putts. The crowd was letting him know that he did not grieve alone, nor would he have to live alone with memories of Renay.

Death. It's a frightening word. Part of what makes it so scary is that we know so little about it. You've probably heard stories about people who have died on the hospital operating table and then come back to life. But most of the information these individuals have reported only further complicates an already confusing subject.

What do we really know about death? The Bible says, "And inasmuch as it is appointed for men to die once and after this comes judgment" (Hebrews 9:27). From this verse, we can be sure of at least three truths.

First, everybody is going to die sooner or later. When

PGA champion Paul Azinger was told that he had cancer, the reality of death set in on him for the first time. In his book, *Zinger,* Paul recalled: "As I lay on the table in that cold, dark room, stripped of all the elements everyone associated with my supposed success, the thought struck me, I could die from this cancer! And suddenly the reality hit me: I am going to die eventually anyhow. Whether from cancer or something else, I am definitely going to die. It is only a question of when.

"When you are thirty-three years of age, hardly sick a day in your life, and sitting on top of the world, you rarely think about dying. Now death was staring me right in the face. Worse still, I sensed that I could die soon. And I was downright scared.

"Beyond that, I suddenly realized that I was not the one in charge. I had long prided myself on steering my own destiny, calling my own shots, and being in control of my life. Now, with just a few puffs of air from a doctor's lips, control was wrenched away from me.

"In that same moment, I recalled some words spoken to me many times by Larry Moody, my spiritual mentor, who directs a Bible study on the PGA Tour. Larry always said, 'Zinger, we are not in the land of the living, going to the land of the dying. We are in the land of the dying, going to the land of the living.' In a much deeper way than ever before, I began to understand what Larry was talking about."[12]

We don't need to get all bent out of shape about it, but realize that we have approximately seventy-five years on this earth, barring any unforeseen accidents or divine appointments. We should enjoy life. Make the best of it. And if we are smart, like Zinger, we will also prepare to die. Insurance policies, wills, cemetery plots, and caskets seem so irrelevant. Yet they are simply acknowledgments of the obvious. Someday we are going to die. The big question is this: What about after death? Are we prepared for that?

Another certainty we have concerning death is this: After death comes God's judgment (Hebrews 9:27). Here is a profound thought to contemplate: We are all going to live forever; the only difference is whether we spend eternity in heaven or hell. This life is not the end. The Bible clearly indicates that we will stand before God in judgment to give an account of what we have done with our lives.

A third certainty concerning death is this: We know that Jesus has beaten death and will return to earth for those who eagerly await Him (Hebrews 9:28). Of course, those who are not looking forward to His return are going to have to face Him, too. A person may succeed in avoiding Christ in this life, but nobody will be able to hide from Him on Judgment

Day. If He is coming to you as a stranger and judge, you should rightfully shudder with terror. But if you know Jesus as your Savior and Friend, that day will be a time of celebration, joy, and excitement.

PRAYER
Life is frightening enough at times, O Lord.
Please help me to have confidence in You
that not only assures me of Your presence
with me in this world,
but in the next as well.

FURTHER READING
1 Corinthians 15:50–58; 2 Corinthians 5:10;
Romans 14:10–12

THE GREEN YOU DON'T
WANT TO HIT

For where jealousy and selfish ambition exist,
there is disorder and every evil thing.
JAMES 3:16

Brent and Steve were good friends. . .until they started playing golf together. Every time they met at the course, Steve
turned green with envy as Brent pulled his shiny new Mer-
cedes sports coupe into the parking lot. Steve bristled as Brent
tipped the boy at the bag drop after he had unloaded his Calla-
way titaniums onto a cart. By the time they actually got onto
the course, Steve was already beaten. Envy and jealousy were

eating him alive.

Nevertheless, he was obsessed with proving that he was a better golfer than Brent. He contended every shot, never conceding a "gimme" on any green, disputing pica-yune points about the rules of play, and in general being a royal pain. Steve's competitive spirit went far beyond the boundaries of good golf etiquette. For him, it was "win at all costs, even if you have to cheat." Eventually, Brent refused to play with Steve. "I didn't come out here to get frustrated," Brent told him. "I came out to enjoy playing golf. I can get frustrated at work."

Ironically, because of Steve's envy and jealousy, the game that could have helped cement their relationship drove the two friends apart.

Envy and jealousy. What a deadly combination! They can kill any relationship. They can destroy a friendship, a business, or a marriage. They can cause two lovers' ardor to slowly slip away.

Technically, envy is wanting what someone else has, while jealousy is a fear of losing something you have. Usually, though, where you find one, you will find the other, along with a soupy mixture of anger, insecurity, resentment, loneliness, selfishness, and pride. Jealousy and envy are the inevitable by-products of a society given over to narcissism.

They are the dubious distinctions of the "me" generation.

Surprisingly, some forms of jealousy are permissible and even appropriate. When, for example, you are jealous for God's honor and glory, that is a good form of jealousy. For His part, God is jealous over His people. He loves us and won't stand idly by while Satan attempts to trip us up or steal us away.

Jealousy is most often negative, though, because we are more concerned about our reputations than we are God's. Jealousy grows out of selfishness and possessiveness and is the direct result of a poor self-image. This attitude charges to the fore when a threat approaches our position, prestige, or something else we deem as our personal domain. We can sense this sort of rivalry when new neighbors move onto our street, when the boss hires another employee, or our spouse looks twice at someone of the opposite sex. And yes, we can find green all over the golf course when someone bests us at our game.

In the Scriptures, jealousy caused King Saul to become a man driven by a phobia. He was afraid of losing his kingdom to David, a young, up-and-comer on the leader board. When the young shepherd slew the giant Goliath with only a slingshot and a few pebbles, Saul was thrilled.

But when the women came out in droves to honor their

new hero, Saul's joy turned to jealousy. It was tough enough for Saul to see and hear the women singing and dancing in the streets, joyfully playing their tambourines and other musical instruments. But when they began chanting, "Saul has slain his thousands and David his ten thousands" (1 Samuel 18:7), it was like rubbing salt in Saul's wounds.

Saul took their praise of David as a personal insult and was suspicious of the young hero from that day on. He even tried to kill David as a result of his jealousy and fear (v. 12). He was so threatened by this newcomer that for the remainder of his rule, Saul regarded David as a rival and was preoccupied with attempts to assassinate his successor.

How can we cope with jealousy? For one thing, we must see it for what it is: a sin. It is not simply a personality quirk; it is wrong. We can ask God to forgive us, to deliver us, and to give us power over it. It doesn't help to keep beating up on ourselves. Remember, most jealousy is the result of an inferiority complex, and condemning ourselves will only frustrate our attempts to overcome jealousy.

Second, we can attempt to understand our rivals better. We can pray for and, if possible, with the people we feel jealous of. By communicating with our rivals, we often alleviate the source of our tension. If not, at least we can see these people as struggling human beings rather than as threats to our security.

Third, we can seek to develop a strong, positive self-image. People with high self-esteem are rarely jealous. They can cry with those who cry and rejoice with those who rejoice. Individuals with good self-concepts know that their success is dependent upon the Lord, not on what other people may or may not accomplish.

PRAYER
Father, help me to remember that
You are doing a good work in and through me.
May I be content with who I am,
and comfortable with how
You are blessing others, as well.

FURTHER READING
1 Samuel 18:5–19

FREE PLAY

*If therefore the Son shall make you free,
you shall be free indeed.*
JOHN 8:36

Next time you are walking up a fairway, pause for a moment, gaze at the beauty around you, and thank God that you live in a land where you can enjoy the freedom to spend your time and money playing golf. Freedom is a precious commodity. It usually comes with a high price tag and it must be guarded carefully if it is not to be lost or taken away.

But have you ever noticed that some people are in prisons of their own making? It does them little good to live in a free country if they are personally bound by guilt, ropes of insecurity, or any other self-imposed limitations on what God has created them to be. Thankfully, Jesus came to set us free—free from sin, but also free to enjoy life with Him.

To be fully enjoyed, however, freedom must be personal. It does us little good to be able to admire the freedom others enjoy if we are still personally bound, if we cannot enter in and participate the way we would like. Yet many Christians live in that sand trap. They gaze wishfully at other believers who seem so uninhibited in their spiritual lives, Christians who are experiencing the grace of God out in the middle of the fairway, planning their next approach shot. Meanwhile, Christians who remain trapped by tradition or in the rough of legalism languish in loneliness, wondering all the while if this is really the victorious life Jesus died to purchase for us.

Why? Because the freedom Christ provides must be appropriated by every individual believer. Otherwise, we remain bound.

In the Bible, we find an account in which Jesus' friend Lazarus had died. He had been dead for four days and had already been buried by the time Jesus arrived on the scene. Of course, Jesus could have arranged to have been at the grave sooner—Lazarus's sisters, Mary and Martha, had contacted Jesus about the situation—but He intentionally had not done so. He could have prevented the death of Lazarus in the first place, a point not lost on the dead man's grieving sisters when they greeted Jesus upon His arrival.

For His part, Jesus was not distracted by any of those details. Not even a loud crowd of mourners around the grave site could deter Jesus. He approached the tomb, a cave covered by a large rock, and said, "Remove the stone."

Against the protests and warnings from the family members and bystanders, the tomb was unsealed. Then in a loud voice, Jesus cried out, "Lazarus, come forth!" and literally called the dead man back to life (John 11:43). Imagine the hush that must have covered that crowd as they waited to see what would happen next.

Someone must have heard a sound from inside the cave. Imagine the anticipation as they watched, too afraid to hope, as Lazarus, still wrapped up like a mummy with even his face draped in cloth, shuffled into the open air. What an outburst there must have been among the people, some no doubt gasping from stark terror, others rejoicing that the loved one they had buried was now upright and breathing.

Jesus, however, proceeded with what was important for Lazarus. The first thing Jesus commanded concerning the man raised from the dead was, "Unbind him, and let him go" (v. 44).

Think about that. Lazarus had been called from death to newness of life, but he was still bound and needed to be set free. Many Christians are walking around like Lazarus when he first came from the tomb. They are saved from death, destruction, and eternal hell, but they are still spiritually bound by their past, tradition, friends' opinions, reputation, or attitude. They need to be set free.

Can you imagine Lazarus's life if he had not been set free? He'd have gone through the rest of his days as a human mummy. He may as well have remained dead!

But that was not Jesus' plan for Lazarus, and it is not His will for us, either. Jesus wants us to be free indeed! Today, accept the fact that you are not only saved, but also accept the truth that Jesus has set you free to be the unique person that God planned for you to be. Shake off any of the grave clothes you might still be wearing and start walking, talking, and living in the true freedom Christ provides.

PRAYER
Lord, help me to accept the gift of freedom that was purchased by the blood of Christ on Calvary. For me to live at a level so far below my calling would be an insult to that cross, so I choose now to believe that I am no longer bound. May I walk with You day by day in the Spirit, undaunted by human categories, institutions, or self-imposed limitations on what You want me to be.

FURTHER READING
John 8:31–59; 11:1–45

HONESTY IN
ALL THINGS

*Pray for us: for we trust we
have a good conscience,
in all things willing to live honestly.*
HEBREWS 13:18 KJV

Picture this: You are in town on business and decide to check out the local links before you leave. You find a good public course, set a tee time, and secure accurate directions. You arrive in plenty of time and are getting ready to tee off when a fellow asks to join you. You graciously consent, acknowledging that you would enjoy the company. The man is a total stranger to you, the two of you have never before met or played golf together, and it is unlikely that you will ever see each other again. You have nothing to prove to each other and you are not playing for money.

On the first hole, you double bogey a par four. As you are marking down a six on your scorecard, you inquire of your partner how many strokes he had taken.

"Gimme a six," he replies.

A six! You shout to yourself. Are you kidding? Although you hadn't really been paying much attention to your fellow player as he slashed his way through the rough and up the fairway, you could almost be sure that he had hit at least eight times before getting the ball on the green. A six, indeed!

From then on, you keep a mental note of your partner's strokes. It didn't really matter to you what he scored; after all, you'd probably never play with this person again, but it nonetheless surprised you when he shaved a stroke or two off nearly every hole he played. . .on the scorecard, that is.

Why would anyone cheat when it didn't matter? If you had been competing against one another, cheating might be understandable, although certainly not acceptable. But why cheat when nothing is at stake?

The truth is that something is always at stake, and that which is at stake is the truth. Nowadays, we are much too willing to accept a convenient truth, something that may not be an outright lie but is not exactly true, either.

But truth cannot be compromised. It is not a matter of perception or opinion. Some things are right or wrong not because society says so or because situational ethics deems them so under your particular circumstances. Right conduct is worth upholding simply because it is right. The truth is absolutely true, and anything less than that is false.

In our hypothetical—yet all too real—story, no doubt your playing partner was not trying to fool you; he was trying to fool himself. He was attempting to dupe himself into believing that he was a better golfer than he really was. He refused to assess himself accurately and found it easier to mark down false information on the scorecard, hoping that somehow the untrue could miraculously become true.

It never does. Lies and half-truths are always found out —if not here in this life, then most certainly when we stand before the One who is absolute Truth.

An intriguing story in the Old Testament illustrates the dangers of lying, both to ourselves and to others. Naaman was the commander of the army of the king of Syria. But Naaman had a serious problem; he had leprosy, a dreaded skin disease that almost always leads to death (2 Kings 5:1). People with leprosy were shunned by the rest of the population.

Imagine what an incredible act of faith (not to mention humility) it was on Naaman's part to seek help from Elisha the prophet, an Israelite living in Samaria under the thumb of Syrian rule. But when Naaman, accompanied by the pomp and pride of his military procession, arrived at Elisha's home, the prophet didn't come out to greet him. Instead, Elisha sent his servant, Gehazi, to deliver instructions concerning how Naaman might be cleansed of his leprosy.

Naaman was furious. No doubt, he anticipated that the prophet would put on some sort of spiritual show for him (v. 11). The one thing he did not expect was to be ignored. Eventually Naaman's servants convinced him to give Elisha's plan a try. After all, if the prophet had asked him to do something difficult, he would have done it, but all Elisha had told him to do was to dip seven times in the Jordan River. What did he have to lose?

When Naaman complied, he was immediately cleansed of his leprosy. Overjoyed at his new lease on life, Naaman wanted to give Elisha a reward for his services. The prophet refused. He was not in the ministry for money.

When Elisha's servant Gehazi heard his master turn down what was likely to be a lucrative reward, his greed got the best of him. No doubt he thought something such as, *Hey, maybe the old man doesn't want anything from Naaman, but I could sure use a few things!* At his first opportunity, Gehazi ran after Naaman, who had started on his way back home. Gehazi caught up to Naaman's caravan and told the commander a lie, that two "Bible school" students had just shown up at Elisha's place and were in need. Could Naaman please give them a talent of silver and a couple changes of clothing?

Naaman gladly handed over the gifts, and Gehazi hurried home to hide them. Then he went back to Elisha.

When Elisha asked Gehazi where he had been, the greedy servant lied again. "Oh, nowhere."

The Scripture concludes the story with these stark words: "Then [Elisha] said to him, 'Did not my heart go with you, when the man turned from his chariot to meet you? Is it a time to receive money and to receive clothes and olive groves and vineyards and sheep and oxen and male and female servants? Therefore, the leprosy of Naaman shall cleave to you and to your descendants forever.' So [Gehazi] went out from his presence a leper as white as snow" (2 Kings 5:26–27).

Did you catch that? Not only Gehazi would live the remainder of his life as a leper because of his lying and cheating, but his children and their children down through the generations would be cursed with the disease as well.

Few of us have been cursed with leprosy, but many of us have brought similar destruction to ourselves and to our families by compromising our values, lying to ourselves, and lying to others. There is no way to improve a lie. We can only repent and start over again.

PRAYER

Oh, Lord, please cleanse me of anything
that is not absolutely true and
keep my heart in such a way
that duplicity and compromise
have no place in me.

FURTHER READING
2 Kings 5

HONOR TO WHOM
HONOR IS DUE

The twenty-four elders will fall down
before Him who sits on the throne,
and will worship Him who lives forever and ever,
and will cast their crowns before the throne, saying,
"Worthy art Thou, our Lord and our God, to receive glory
and honor and power; for Thou didst create all things,
and because of Thy will they existed, and were created."
REVELATION 4:10–11

The winner of the Pebble Beach National Pro-Am takes
home a fifty-eight-piece set of Waterford crystal, as well as a

tournament trophy. You may never win at Pebble Beach, but you, too, probably have some trophies that you regard as prize possessions. Perhaps you have achieved a high level of success in your career. Maybe you have been honored in school or on the job as a person who does excellent work. Or maybe your community has spotlighted you for your outstanding service to other people. All of these things are noble and worth achieving.

Interestingly, however, all of our worldly honors, titles, degrees, trophies, and awards will pale when we see Jesus face-to-face in heaven. Compared to the honor of knowing and loving Him, nothing else matters. The twenty-four elders in Revelation cast their crowns at Jesus' feet as an indication that His worth and accomplishments far exceeded anything they had to offer. How much more insignificant are our trinkets that we point to as our signs of success?

One day, we will sheepishly toss our most treasured trophies at Jesus' feet. Not that our earthly accolades are of no value to the Lord or to us. They are indeed. But when we realize what little we have to offer Him as tokens of our honor and esteem for Him, we will be humbled by how He has honored us, even by allowing us in His presence.

Some people, in their sincere attempts to express their feelings of gratitude to the Lord, say such things as, "When I get to heaven, I'm going to go right up to Jesus and thank Him for dying on the cross for me."

That sounds impressive, but it is totally unrealistic. When the apostle John saw simply a vision of Jesus in heaven, he was overpowered by the awesome presence of the glorified Christ. Remember, John was one of Jesus' closest friends during the time He walked the earth. John was perhaps the disciple who Jesus loved most tenderly. Yet when John saw Jesus in heaven, the apostle reported, "And when I saw Him, I fell at His feet as a dead man" (Revelation 1:17).

All of our earthly honors, accomplishments, trophies, and successes will seem suddenly insignificant compared to knowing Jesus as Lord. Keeping that in mind now will help us to set proper priorities and to keep our achievements in perspective.

PRAYER
Lord, help me to see all of my earthly accomplishments
as crowns that I will one day cast at Your feet.
Please give me wisdom to know which of those things
that I value in this life will hold their value in eternity.

FURTHER READING
Revelation 1:4–18

HOW MUCH
IS ENOUGH?

For the love of money is a root of all sorts of evil,
and some by longing for it have
wandered away from the faith,
and pierced themselves with many a pang.
1 TIMOTHY 6:10

Have you ever dreamed about being a professional golfer? Imagine, playing a game you love and making money while you do it! What could be better? Winning just one tournament could land you almost half a million dollars. What a life!

In truth, of course, while those players who consistently

soar to the top of the money list are multimillionaires, many professional golfers are barely eking out a living after paying their expenses. Many pros playing on the Nike Tour, the European Tour, and other circuits never achieve financial success.

But how much money do you need to consider yourself a financial success? How much is enough to make you happy? Sadly, some people, no matter how much money and material success they have, cannot purchase happiness.

Do you remember Imelda Marcos, the former first lady of the Philippines (until her husband's exile in 1986)? The woman may have given new meaning to the term "expensive tastes." Concerning Mrs. Marcos, New York congressman Stephen Solarz once quipped, "Compared to her, Marie Antoinette was a bag lady."[13]

When the Marcoses were forced to hurriedly escape their personal palace paradise, Imelda left behind 2,700 pairs of shoes, 1,500 Gucci and other name-brand handbags, more than 1,200 designer gowns (each worn only once), and 35 large standing clothes racks, loaded with expensive fur coats.

Spending money was almost an obsession for Imelda. The figures on her material largess are staggering. Talk about going on a shopping spree! During one trip to Kenya, Iraq, and New York, Imelda blew $1.5 million. She took home 20 trunks full of trinkets and 500 boxes of macadamia nut candies. On a trip to Rome, Copenhagen, and New York, Mrs. Marcos squandered $7 million in ninety days. She spent $10.3 million on her daughter's wedding. She once bought $2,000 worth of chewing gum while simply passing through the San Francisco airport!

Whether because of greed, foolishness, or a vain attempt to destroy the memories of her poor childhood, Imelda's possessions became an obsession. Said one of her press aides, "In the beginning, Imelda merely collected possessions. In the end, she became possessed by them."

Something similar can happen to any of us. While most of us will not have the material possessions of Imelda Marcos or the staggering income of Tiger Woods, the quest for more and more money can consume us.

Understand, there's nothing wrong with having money or the things money can buy. But when money accompanied by materialism (the lust for things) has us, we are in big trouble.

Jesus talked a lot about money. In fact, He talked more about our relationship to money and material things than He did many other subjects. In the heart of a discussion about what it means to be a dedicated disciple, Jesus said, "For what does it profit a man to gain the whole world, and forfeit his soul? For what shall a man give in exchange for his soul?" (Mark 8:36–37). Jesus is saying if we could get the entire world, but we lost our souls in doing so, it would be a bad deal.

We don't usually see the issue so starkly; rarely do we get such black-and-white comparisons to study. Satan normally attempts to dull the thrust of Jesus' words by painting these contrasts in various shades of gray and beige. But there it is. Jesus is straightforwardly warning us that nothing in this world is worth losing our relationship with Him.

Maybe that's why He instructed us, "Do not lay up for yourselves treasures upon earth, where moth and rust destroy, and where thieves break in and steal. But lay up for yourselves treasures in heaven, where neither moth nor rust destroys, and where thieves do not break in or steal; for where your treasure is, there will your heart be also" (Matthew 6:19–21). In other words, if we invest in the things that are important to God, our investments will be waiting for us in heaven. . .with interest. But if we focus on acquiring more of this world's goods simply to lavish upon ourselves, we will literally "live it up."

Working hard and making a profitable living are admirable goals. The key, of course, is to learn how to be content. If our satisfaction and contentment are based on materialism, we will be on a constant quest for more. Make up your mind to put

Jesus ahead of your material possessions and the fleeting security of popular success.

PRAYER

Father, whether I have a lot or a little of
what this world regards as material success,
let me use whatever I have
for Your honor and glory.
And may I find peace and contentment
in knowing that You will provide all I really need.

FURTHER READING
Mark 8:34–38; 1 Timothy 6:3–19

A REAL WINNER

For God so loved the world,
that He gave His only begotten Son,
that whoever believes in Him should not perish,
but have eternal life.
JOHN 3:16

As a third-string member of his high school football team, Tom sat on the bench and watched throughout the season while his teammates fought their way to and won the state championship. Tom had not contributed much to the team's success. In fact, he had not played in a single game all season, not even for a single down!

Recalling that awful feeling of seeing his friends

enjoying success while he was not, Tom said, "I felt like a failure, like I didn't belong on the team. I felt worthless, empty, and lonely. These were feelings that had followed me all my life. I was searching for something, but I didn't know what. The football victory only made the feelings stronger—like I didn't measure up."

Worse yet, Tom began to feel totally insignificant, that his life was a joke. "I felt guilty," he said, "because I wanted to be a good kid. I wanted to be a good athlete. But I could never measure up. I was never good enough. I felt like I didn't matter. I remember asking some pretty deep questions for a fifteen-year-old. Why am I here? What gives life meaning? Why am I so miserable?"

It wasn't until Tom attended a Fellowship of Christian Athletes meeting that he began to find the answers to his questions. Tom recalls that the athletes at that meeting were not discussing the big game or their latest accomplishments in sports. They were talking about such unusual topics as "unconditional love" and "eternal acceptance."

That's what I need! Tom thought.

The student athletes explained to Tom that God had sent Jesus, His only Son, to die on a cross to save Tom from his sins.

Tom was amazed. "This is incredible! You're telling me that God did that for me—someone who doesn't matter? He loved me enough to do that?"

For the first time in his life, Tom Lehman felt that he really did matter—he mattered to God. That night, he prayed and trusted Jesus Christ as his Savior. Tom committed his life to Christ and began an exciting relationship with the Lord.

In 1996, Tom Lehman won his first major, the British Open, and became the first American ever to win the tourney at the Royal Lytham and St. Anne's course. In his remarks as he accepted the Claret Jug, Lehman said, "I really believe God loves all of us. . .I know He cares about me. I know He cares about you."[14]

PRAYER
God, you are so big, and I am so small.
You are so awesome, so incomprehensible,
and I am so insignificant in
the overall scheme of this world.
Yet You love me, even me!
Give me a fresh understanding, Father,
of just how much You really do care about me.

FURTHER READING
John 1:1–18; 20:30–31

SLOW PLAY

For am I now seeking the favor of men, or of God?
GALATIANS 1:10

Few things are more frustrating on the golf course than having to disrupt our rhythm by waiting for the players in front of us who are taking an interminable amount of time to negotiate even the simplest of shots. We pace impatiently on the tee as the players ahead of us hack their way through the course, their drives dribbling off the tee a distance of fifty yards, fairway shots skittering in every direction.

Occasionally, we cast a long, accusing shadow over the players ahead of us by hitting a ball that lands dangerously close to them. But such aggressive play is usually counterproductive.

After all, it's tough to keep our mind on our game when we silently scream before each shot, "Okay, you dunderclunks, here I come! Get out of the way!"

Slow play can be especially exasperating when we are playing well. . .or playing poorly. We want to get on with our game and try to make something happen. Making matters worse, we may find ourselves following a mixed foursome: men teeing off from the blue or white tees, women hitting from the reds. More time spent waiting.

Meanwhile, back on the tee, we are fuming. When we finally feel that it is safe to hit, we blast our tee shot. . .into oblivion: the nearest thatch of trees or the deepest pond within reach. Slow play. It can drive us bonkers.

On the other hand, many amateurs attempt to play too quickly. They worry so much about the players behind them that they nervously dub one shot after another as they rush to get out of the way. Certainly, we should always maintain a high level of golf etiquette. It is, after all, golf. If we are consistently playing more slowly than the players behind us, we can simply step aside for a few minutes and allow them to play through. Both their game and our game will improve as a result.

Playing golf well, however, takes a bit of time. We must concentrate on every stroke, and we can't do that if we are worrying about somebody behind us. We may be surprised to discover that by taking our time, concentrating on each shot, giving ourselves the best chance we can of success, we actually progress around the course more quickly. Why? Simple. We aren't spending nearly so much time looking for our ball in the rough. By trying to rush the process, we increase our risk of error.

The same is true in our relationship with the Lord. There may be people who get frustrated with us, saying that we are progressing too quickly or too slowly. But sound spiritual growth takes time, and the process cannot be rushed. The apostle Paul spent fourteen years or more learning the things of God before he began to take a more public role in the early church. Allow God the time it takes to develop His character in you. Study. Prepare. Concentrate. Focus on those things that are important, and don't worry; your time will come.

PRAYER
Father, I know the opinions of my peers
can be fickle and often foolish.
Let me always strive to please You rather than other people.
Let me grow in Your grace according to Your timetable for me.

FURTHER READING
Galatians 1:10–2:2

THE COURSE
ALWAYS WINS

For by grace you have been saved through faith;
and that not of yourselves,
it is the gift of God;
not as a result of works,
that no one should boast.
EPHESIANS 2:8–9

Nobody has ever mastered the game of golf. Just about the time you think you have it all together, one day you go out on the course, and you can't seem to find where you left it. At the height of his playing career, golf analyst and television announcer Johnny Miller suddenly plunged from number two on the money list to fourteenth, to forty-eighth the following year, to 111th the next. He played for ten more years yet never again cracked the top ten. No matter what adjustments to his swing Miller made, what new technique he tried, what new equipment he used, Johnny Miller couldn't win.

Something similar happened to the legendary Jack Nicklaus. In 1979, at age thirty-nine, the Golden Bear suddenly dropped to seventy-first on the money list. He rebounded in the years to follow, but for awhile, even the game's greatest player felt as though he might never win again.

The truth is, no matter how well or how badly we play, the course always wins.

Nobody truly masters the course.

Similarly, nobody ever masters the game of life. We may work hard, do all the right things, but guess what? We probably won't get out of here alive. Nor will we ever master the course during this lifetime. We all fail to perform at peak levels. At our best we are inconsistent. If there is anything we are consistent about, it is our inconsistency! We blow shots every day. We miss opportunities. We do things that we should not and don't do many of the things we should.

Ironically, when many people are asked the question: "On what basis do you hope to go to heaven?" the most frequent response is, "I've been a good person."

Oh, really? According to the Bible, none of us are good enough to merit heaven.

Quoting from the Old Testament books of Isaiah and Psalms, the apostle Paul penned a description that sounds painfully like us: "As it is written, 'There is none righteous, not even one; there is none who understands, there is none who seeks for God; all have turned aside, together they have become useless; there is none who does good, there is not even one. Their throat is an open grave, with their tongues they keep deceiving, the poison of asps is under their lips; Whose mouth is full of cursing and bitterness; Their feet are swift to shed blood, destruction and misery are in their paths, and the path of peace have they not known. There is no fear of God before their eyes' " (Romans 3:10–18).

Paul concluded this portion of his discussion with the sad statement, "For all have sinned and fall short of the glory of God" (Romans 3:23). The Greek word used for "sin" more often than any other in the New Testament is *hamartia,* which means "to miss the mark," or as Paul puts it, to fall short.

It's as though we are attempting to reach the green in regulation, and to do so, we must hit our shot so it clears a pond in front of the green. We give it our best effort, but we don't quite make it, and our golf ball falls short, lost in a dark pool of deep water. That is the biblical concept of sin. At our very best, we are not good enough to make heaven. The course is too tough.

That's why, of course, you should put your trust and faith in the one Person who has mastered life's course, Jesus Christ. Let Him be your Master. Allow Him to make the shots for you.

PRAYER

It is a very humbling realization, Lord,
when I recognize that even at my best,
I can never be good enough to earn my way to heaven.
The concept of being saved by grace
grates against my sense of self-determination.
Yet at the same time,
I am grateful that I do not have to
stand before You on my own merit,
that Jesus' death on the cross did for me
what I could not accomplish for myself.
Thank You, Lord, for Your amazing gift.

FURTHER READING
Ephesians 2:1–10

PLAY TO WIN,
BUT IF YOU DON'T. . .

And everyone who competes in the games
exercises self-control in all things.
They then do it to receive a perishable wreath,
but we an imperishable.
1 CORINTHIANS 9:25

In a professional golf tournament, there is really only one winner. Sure, other players who score well and finish high on the leader board take home a check, too, but the title goes to one person.

Ironically, many pro golfers have never won a tournament

on the PGA Tour—not only have they missed winning a major tournament; they haven't won at all! Take Bobby Wadkins, for instance, brother of Ryder Cup Captain, Lanny Wadkins. Bobby has played golf professionally for more than twenty years, entering an average of thirty tournaments each year. But unlike his brother Lanny, to date, Bobby Wadkins has never won a tournament. Nor have many of the other men and women in the middle or lower end of the pack on the PGA and LPGA money lists. Many players have been teeing it up professionally for more than a decade and have yet to take home their first trophy.

Are they losers? Maybe by some people's standards. But many of these midrange players are incredible golfers, making more than half a million dollars a year while playing in the middle of the pack. With endorsements (advertisements and commercials for which they are paid), corporate outings, and speaking engagements, some midrange players nearly double their annual winnings on the course.

In the course of life, the apostle Paul was a realist. He recognized that it wasn't just winning the crown that mattered, but how we play the game. He encouraged Christians at the church in Corinth to do their best. "Do you not know that those who run in a race all run, but only one receives the prize? Run in such a way that you may win" (1 Corinthians 9:24). Yet in the very next breath, Paul instructed all of us to aim well, to work hard, to keep our standards high, whether we are among those at the top or one of those who don't quite have our game together.

Paul wrote, "And everyone who competes in the games exercises self-control in all things. They then do it to receive a perishable wreath, but we an imperishable. Therefore I run in such a way, as not without aim; I box in such a way, as not beating the air; but I buffet my body and make it my slave, lest possibly, after I have preached to others, I myself should be disqualified" (1 Corinthians 9:25–27).

Paul understood that it was not simply the prize that mattered. It was how he conducted himself during the contest. Whether you are the course pro or the course duffer, play your game with all your heart. And keep in mind that in spiritual matters, you are playing for a much more significant prize than a number on a scorecard.

PRAYER

Lord, help me to be disciplined about the way I live,
regardless of whether I am in the limelight
or in the shadows of life.
Let me be ever aware that I am not performing,
not trying to impress a crowd,
but that I am representing You to the world.

FURTHER READING
2 Timothy 2:11

STRAIGHT AHEAD

For the LORD knows the way of the righteous,
But the way of the wicked will perish.
PSALM 1:6

Here's another of those increasingly wild, wacky inventions that is supposed to miraculously transform our golf game: It's called the "Stance Guide," and its simplicity may only be surpassed by the stupidity of people who purchase it.

The Stance Guide is actually a pair of bright-colored adhesive arrows that when applied to the toes of golf shoes —properly applied, of course—will point in the same direction as the intended target line. In other words, you are to go around the golf course (and into the clubhouse, we might assume?)

with two arrows pointing the way to the hole.

This is not a joke. "It's so simple that even I can't believe how well it works," gushes inventor Bob Delgado.[15] One package, including three sets of waterproof, soil-resistant arrows, should last one golf season according to the product's promotional literature. This thing is guaranteed to improve your game.

Yep. And elephants can fly.

Fortunately, when it comes to finding the right direction for our lives, God has not abandoned us to relying upon fluorescent arrows on our shoes. He has promised to direct our paths, to guide us in the right direction if we will trust Him. Proverbs 3:5–6 says, "Trust in the LORD with all your heart, and do not lean on your own understanding. In all your ways acknowledge Him, and He will make your paths straight." That is where we usually stop reading in this passage, but the promise is followed by a strong word of caution: "Do not be wise in your own eyes; fear the Lord and turn away from evil" (v. 7).

One of the easiest ways to avoid evil is to avoid people who welcome evil or tempt us toward wrong things. Maybe that is why the psalmist declared, "How blessed is the man who does not walk in the counsel of the wicked, nor stand in the path of sinners, nor sit in the seat of scoffers! But his delight is in the law of the LORD, and in His law he meditates day and night. . . . For the LORD knows the way of the righteous, but the way of the wicked will perish" (Psalm 1:1–2, 6).

Clearly, walking in the wrong direction, spending the majority of our discretionary time with those who do not share our faith in the Lord, will cause us to make dangerous mistakes. Willfully stepping into the flow of sin rather than into the flow of God's Spirit will lead us to improper thoughts, which will lead to improper conduct, which will result in an improper lifestyle. And guess where that lifestyle will eventually lead? Yep. The ungodly will perish.

On the other hand, if we keep our eyes on the Lord, and keep our thoughts focused on His Word, that too will show up in our conduct and lifestyle. And the path on which He takes us will not only lead to the top of our game, it will point us to an eternal reward in heaven.

PRAYER

Father, I truly want to walk with You. Please keep me on the path that leads to life. Even during those times when I might be tempted to take a different route, or to spend more time with the ungodly elements around me, my desire is to remain on the right road. If Your Holy Spirit must nudge, prod, teach, or correct me, I will welcome whatever is necessary to keep me moving in a heavenly direction.

FURTHER READING
Psalm 1

A TIME TO SPEAK

*For if you remain silent at this time, relief and deliverance
will arise for the Jews from another place and you
and your father's house will perish. And who knows whether
you have not attained royalty for such a time as this?*
ESTHER 4:14

Every golfer who knows anything about golf etiquette knows
that there is a time to speak while on the course and a time
to keep silent. When another player is teeing off, for example, silence is golden. Or when your partner is putting, conversation is inappropriate.

Certainly, part of the pleasure of a round of golf with
friends, family, or business associates is the conversation and

friendly competitive banter exchanged between players. But golfers who talk when they should be quiet or who chatter non-stop throughout the round run the risk of either having their mouths stuffed with other players' golf balls or playing by themselves.

On the other hand, there are times that, if we want to comply with the rules of golf, we must speak up. For instance, when we dub a shot or hit it into what may be some out-of-bounds location, we can legally hit a provisional ball, a second shot which is considered in play until it is determined that our first shot is out of play. In such a situation, before hitting our next shot, we must announce to our fellow players, "I'm going to hit a provisional ball." In doing so, we say, "This is a just-in-case-I-can't-find-my-ball shot."

If we don't speak up, our fellow players have a right to assume that our second ball is the one we are now playing—that we have accepted the fact that our first ball has gone to golf ball heaven, that we have given ourselves one penalty stroke, and that we are now content to play the second shot where it lies.

Another situation often ignored by amateurs, but never by professionals, is that if we believe our ball is too scuffed, scratched, cut, severely dented, or otherwise unfit for play, we must tell our fellow players before we pick up the ball to inspect it. And we must let them observe our inspection and see the ball for themselves before we remove it from play and replace it with another. Finally, we must ask their permission to remove the ball. Failure to speak up about replacing our ball could lead to penalty strokes and possibly disqualification in a serious tournament.

Failure to speak up for what is right whether on the golf course, at home, or in the public arena is always dangerous. Silence may be golden, but it can also be costly. In the Bible, a beautiful young woman named Esther was faced with just such a decision: Should she speak up and risk her life, or could she possibly keep quiet, go with the flow, and still maintain her integrity?

Reading the story of Esther is a real treat. It has more excitement and intrigue than a TV miniseries. It's about sex, money, power, and betrayal. The heroine could easily have been known as "Miss Persia," since she had won a contest held to find a wife for King Ahasuerus, also known as King Xerxes. The Bible calls attention to the fact that "the young lady was beautiful of form and face" (Esther 2:7), and her natural beauty, charm, and grace so impressed King Xerxes that he crowned her queen of Persia.

But there was a problem. In Xerxes' administration lurked an evil, intolerably arrogant, manipulative man named Haman, who hatched a plot to have all the Jews who were living in Persia annihilated. Little did the king know when he gave his approval to Haman's henchmen that Queen Esther was of Jewish background!

Using a combination of beauty, brains, and boldness, Esther turned the tables on Haman. But not before her cousin Mordecai had to remind her that sometimes a person must stand up and be counted, regardless of the cost. At the risk of death, Esther decided, "I will go. . .and if I perish, I perish" (4:16). Esther's courage saved her own life as well as the lives of her people. As for Haman, he ended up hanging from the gallows he had built for Mordecai.

It won't always be easy to stand up for what is right, to speak out when it would be safer to remain silent. But there are times when we have to trust the Lord to give us the courage, to give us the right words, to give us His insight on a matter. . .and then open our mouth and speak out.

PRAYER
Lord, I don't want to spend the majority of my life preparing to live. Please give me the ability to see opportunities to represent You now, not just one of these days. As the challenges come, please give me courage and wisdom about how I can say and do that which will bring the most honor to Your great name.

FURTHER READING
Esther 1–4; Matthew 6:33

WATER BALLS

Now faith is the assurance of things hoped for,
the conviction of things not seen.
HEBREWS 11:1

Do you believe in predestination? Sure you do. . .if you're a golfer. As one who has failed to negotiate a few water hazards, you know in your heart of hearts that some golf balls are simply predestined to spend their lives on the bottom of ponds—especially those balls that you have dubbed your "water balls."

Most golf courses include their fair share of water hazards. Some courses in areas that receive a lot of rain have as many as nine to twelve creeks, lakes, or ponds which must be eluded as you make your way around an eighteen-hole course.

And that's to say nothing of golf courses in Bermuda, Hawaii, or along the California coastline at which the ocean is considered a water hazard!

Think of your least favorite water hazard. If you are like many golfers, your worst wet nemesis is a pond that lies directly in front of a tee area. That pond sucks up your golf balls faster than Titlest can make them. No doubt you have probably witnessed that pond stretch in width or length, just to catch one of your tee shots.

Of course, the problem is not with the pond's size, shape, or location; the problem is in your mind. You come off the green, feeling good about the putt you just poured into the hole, and there, staring you in the face is your worst fear.

Oh, no! you think. *A water hole. I hate teeing off over water!* You look lovingly at the beautiful new golf ball you are playing. *I certainly don't want to hit this baby into the lake,* you lament to yourself. What to do? *These things cost too much money just to knock them into the water,* you continue to worry. Finally you hit upon a solution.

You go back to your golf bag and dig out the oldest, dirtiest, cheapest, and most cut-up golf ball you can find. "I'm not taking any chances of losing a good ball to this water," you announce esoterically to your playing partners. "I'm going to hit my water ball!"

Your fellow players all nod in understanding, marveling at your infinite wisdom.

You step up to the tee, check your alignment, take a practice swing, and address the ball.

Whoosh! goes your golf club.

Sploosh! goes your water ball, right where you had imagined it might. You tip your visor in a brief commemorative ceremony for your ball before you head toward the drop area. You have buried another one in the sea of forgetfulness.

Does that scenario sound all too familiar? The truth is that our minds are amazing computers, but they cannot deal with a negative command. When we tell ourselves, "Don't hit the ball into the water," our subconscious mind only receives the message, "Hit the ball into the water!"

If we want our ball to avoid getting wet, we need to think something like, *I want to drop this shot right out there on the fairway, about seventy-five yards in front of the green.* We must say what we want to have happen, rather than what we don't want.

This principle holds true in every area of life. It's amazing how differently our kids or coworkers respond when we tell them what we expect them to do, rather than warning them against something. Similarly, our own actions are different when we picture ourselves succeeding at what we want to do, rather than allowing ourselves to entertain thoughts of failure. God wants to help us, but we must put our faith in Him. Scripture says, "And without faith it is impossible to please Him, for he who comes to God must believe that He is, and that He is a rewarder of those who seek Him" (Hebrews 11:6).

Our faith in God and in the abilities He has given us will help bring our plans to fruition. Real faith is not simply believing in that which we see; real faith trusts the One who sees the future to bring to pass that for which we are believing.

PRAYER
May my spiritual eyes see You, Jesus,
and having once seen You,
may my faith abound to believe
for Your best in my life.

FURTHER READING
Hebrews 11

CONFIDENCE IN
THE FACE OF CONFLICT

*As they observed
the confidence of Peter and John,
and understood that they were
uneducated and untrained men,
they were marveling,
and began to recognize them as
having been with Jesus.*
ACTS 4:13

Confidence is an essential element to a successful golf game.
That inner strength is especially important when confronting

a challenging situation. In *Mulligan's Laws,* a very tongue-in-cheek look at golf, writer Henry Beard presents seven principles which you may want to keep in the back of your mind when you are in a tough spot on the links. According to *Mulligan's Laws:*

1. Bets lengthen putts and shorten drives.
2. Confidence evaporates in the presence of water.
3. In the heat of a match, balls tend to rise to the surface of the rough.
4. It takes considerable pressure to make a penalty stroke adhere to a scorecard.
5. No matter how much energy you expend, it's impossible to lower the stakes or raise your handicap.
6. Over time, any putter can reach a temperature of absolute zero.
7. If the loss is sufficiently infuriating, matter can be destroyed.[16]

While Beard's insights are interesting, a more astounding example of confidence can be found in Acts 3–4. You'll probably want to read the entire account for yourself, but here's the story in a nutshell.

About two months after the death and resurrection of Christ, Peter and John, two of Jesus' closest friends during His ministry on earth, were going up to the Jewish temple to pray. Outside one of the main gates to the temple area, the apostles encountered a lame beggar sitting near the entry. The beggar hit on Peter and John, asking them for a few bucks to support his favorite charity. . .himself. But Peter and John looked him right in the eyes, and Peter said, "I do not possess silver and gold, but what I do have I give to you: In the name of Jesus Christ the Nazarene—walk!" (Acts 3:6).

And the guy got up and walked. Actually, he did much more than walk. He began "walking and leaping and praising God" all the way into the temple, along with Peter and John (v. 8). The local worshipers recognized the beggar, and they were amazed that he had been healed (v. 10). After all, the man was more than forty years old (v. 22), and he probably had been crippled most or all of those years. No doubt, he had become a fixture outside the gate of the temple. People pitied him—contributing a few coins—or despised him and avoided his desperate, despairing stare. Now here he was, right in the temple of the Lord, dancing and praising God. Did the people notice? Count on it.

The apostle Peter explained the miracle to the crowd:

"Men of Israel, why do you marvel at this, or why do you gaze at us, as if by our own power or piety we had made him walk? The God of Abraham, Isaac, and Jacob, the God of our fathers, has glorified His servant Jesus. . . . The one whom God raised from the dead, a fact to which we are witnesses. And on the basis of faith in His name, it is the name of Jesus which has strengthened this man whom you see and know; and the faith which comes through Him has given him this perfect health in the presence of you all."

ACTS 3:12–13, 15–16

While the crowd may have been impressed with Peter's message, the Jewish rulers were not. They had Peter and John hauled into prison for telling people about Jesus. The next day, the apostles were called to give an account of themselves before Annas, Caiaphas, John, and Alexander, the same chief priests who had condemned Jesus to death less than two months previously! The Jewish leaders asked, "By what power, or in what name, have you done this?" (Acts 4:7).

The Jewish rulers were probably not expecting Peter's response: "Let it be known to all of you, and to all the people of Israel, that by the name of Jesus Christ the Nazarene, whom you crucified, whom God raised from the dead—by this name this man stands here before you in good health. . . . And there is salvation in no one else; for there is no other name under heaven that has been given among men, by which we must be saved" (vv. 10, 12).

Talk about confidence! Peter was saying precisely what the Jewish chiefs did not want to hear. Still, the priests could not deny that something was different about these guys. Can't you imagine those stuffy, old chief priests' expressions as they listened to Peter's words? No doubt, they wondered, *Who are these jokers anyhow? How dare they say such things to us, the cream of the religious crop! Who do these guys think they are?*

But then they began to recognize the apostles as having been with Jesus.

"Where do they get their confidence?"

"They have been with Jesus."

"How do they know so much? They've never gone to Bible school or seminary. How can they understand these things?"

"They have been with Jesus."

"Where did they get such power?"

"They have been with Jesus."

That says it all, doesn't it? They have been with Jesus. They have been spending time in His presence. They are filled with His Holy Spirit and convinced that Jesus Christ is alive from the dead. They are unstoppable.

If you really want confidence in your spiritual life, spend time in the presence of the Lord. People will recognize something different about you, but more importantly, you will know the secret to the confident Christian life.

PRAYER
Oh, that when others observe me
they might think,
"That person has been with Jesus!"

FURTHER READING
Acts 3, 4

ONE SIZE
DOESN'T FIT ALL

"When He, the Spirit of truth, comes,
He will guide you into all truth:
for He will not speak on His own initiative,
but whatever He hears, He will speak;
and He will disclose to you what is to come.
He shall glorify Me;
for He shall take of Mine, and shall disclose it to you."
JOHN 16:13–15

For the traveling golfer who doesn't want to lug a loaded golf bag through the airport or in the trunk of the car, there is at last a solution: the "Super Stick," the one-club miracle tool that is—count 'em—seventeen clubs in one. Better still, the Super Stick is collapsible for easy storage and, ostensibly, easy packing for travel.

Believe it or not, the Super Stick is a real golf club. With a twist of a coin, its stainless steel club head turns into whatever club the shot requires: a driving iron with twelve degrees loft or any of nine normally lofted irons. You also have your choice of three wedges, a chipping iron, and three—who knows why— three putters. The Super Stick's shaft is fitted with a True Temper shaft that locks for play but then is quickly and easily shrunken to twenty-four inches for travel or storage. With this club, one club is all you need.

Unlike the Super Stick, not all Scripture or scriptural principles fit every situation. It is true that "All Scripture is inspired by God and profitable for teaching, for reproof, for correction, for training in righteousness; that the man of God may be adequate, equipped for every good work" (2 Timothy 3:16–17). At the same time, there is much to be said about having a "fitting word in season," in other words, the right scriptural message for the particular situations we or others are facing. God expects us to use common sense and recognize that while all Scripture is true and valuable, not every Scripture is applicable to every circumstance.

The key to using Scripture correctly is to discern what part of God's Word He wants to apply to the current need or circumstances. For that, there is only one method of discovery —practice.

Just as we must practice with all our golf clubs, not just our driver or our putter, we must also practice applying various portions of the Word of God until we know how each portion of Scripture can impact a particular situation. Certainly, there will be times when the Holy Spirit will surprise us. He may use a putter when we would have chosen a wedge, but with experience, we will learn to discern and trust His leading, and we will be amazed at the effectiveness of our scriptural application.

PRAYER

Father, teach me to discern Your voice.
I want to know You so well that
I can sense Your heart as I attempt
to apply scriptural principles
to life's situations.

FURTHER READING
John 14:25–29; 15:26–27; 16:7–15

PLAYING ON EMPTY

Nathan then said to David,
"You are the man! . . .
Why have you despised the word of the LORD
by doing evil in His sight?"
2 SAMUEL 12:7, 9

During a hot day on the golf course, it is easy to become dehydrated. So most experienced players make a habit of drinking from a bottle of water they carry with them or stopping at every water cooler on the course. Similarly if we haven't eaten a good meal before playing, we can feel our energy levels decline as we make our way from tee to tee. Often, bad shots are not due to lack of skill but to a lack of energy. Our concentration may be blown because we are deficient in blood sugar. Eating an apple or a fruit bar midway through the round might just do wonders for our golf score, as well as for our overall enjoyment of the game.

While physical dehydration can be dangerous on a golf course, spiritual dehydration is a very real danger in making our way through life's course. Many sincere Christians allow their personal spiritual reservoirs to run dangerously low. They continue to play on empty physically, emotionally, and spiritually. They continue going and going, doing and doing for God. They constantly are going somewhere or doing something in His name. Either they don't realize their fragile condition, or if they do, they fail to take any steps to rectify it.

Ironically, the most dedicated Christian is frequently the leading candidate for spiritual dryness. Why? Because it is easy to get so busy doing "God's work" that we have little or no time left to enjoy God's presence. Spiritual dehydration usually comes from constantly giving out, but it also results from a failure to adequately replenish our spiritual resources.

The truth is: We can't give out what we don't have. And when we allow ourselves to run dry spiritually, we mess up something much more important than golf shots. Our emptiness may negatively affect our families, friends, coworkers, or employees. Depending on our sphere of influence, dozens, hundreds, possibly even thousands of lives may be negatively impacted by our spiritual dryness.

For a classic example of this, study the life of King David. The first ten chapters of 2 Samuel are mostly chronicles of David's mighty victories on the battlefield. Then comes chapter eleven, one of the most infamous accounts in Scripture: the tragic story of David and Bathsheba.

You probably remember the main event: how David stayed back in Jerusalem while his armies went out to fight; how he was walking around the roof of his home one night and spied beautiful Bathsheba bathing below; how he sent his messengers to bring Bathsheba to him; how he had sex with her, even though both were married to other spouses; how when Bathsheba became pregnant, David attempted to dupe her husband, Uriah, by bringing him home from the battle front in order to sleep with his wife.

When Uriah nobly refused, David sent him back to the front with orders to General Joab to put Uriah in the thick of the fighting and then fall back. David virtually authorized Uriah's murder. After a feigned period of mourning, David added Bathsheba to his collection of wives (he had several already).

How could David, a man after God's own heart, have allowed his heart to become so callous? Easy. David had been working hard since he was a boy. He had been running and fighting since he was a teenager. When he finally became a leader, his schedule and responsibilities did not lessen. They intensified. More battles ensued. Challengers came out of the woodwork. No doubt, by the time of David's adulterous affair with Bathsheba, he was tired physically and empty spiritually. Possibly he had not taken time to replenish his own spiritual reserves. He was so busy fighting for God, he had failed to take time with God. Sound familiar?

It was more than a year before David admitted his moral failure and sin. Confession came only after Nathan the prophet confronted him. When Nathan looked at David and said bluntly, "You are the man!" it was not a compliment; the prophet's statement forced David to acknowledge his sin.

David repented, and God forgave him, but there remained dire consequences for his sin during the rest of the king's life. Sin leaves marks on our lives just like a nail marks a piece of wood. The nail can be removed, the hole patched, but there will always be a scar. Sadly, had King David taken time to replenish his spiritual reserves, the sordid affair might never had happened.

How can we replenish our spiritual energy? There are no secrets: We can easily keep up our reserves through personal Bible study, prayer, fellowship with other believers, or simply by spending time alone with God.

Mark Twain once described golf as "a good walk spoiled," but perhaps a good walk in the woods, or along a beach, or in a park, or at some other quiet place where you can talk with the Lord—and more importantly, listen for His voice—might be the first step to reestablishing your close relationship with God. Keep your spiritual reservoirs full. When you sense that your energy level is low, address that situation immediately. Make whatever changes are necessary in your course management; this is one part of your game that is too important to leave to chance.

PRAYER

Lord, please help me to be sensitive to Your Spirit's promptings to replenish my spiritual reserves. Give me the courage to say no to those things which will continually drain me, and the wisdom to say yes to those things that will refresh me spiritually.

FURTHER READING
2 Samuel 11:1–12:24; Isaiah 40:30–31

ENJOYING THE
NINETEENTH HOLE

If we say that we have fellowship with Him
and yet walk in the darkness,
we lie and do not practice the truth;
but if we walk in the light as He Himself is in the light,
we have fellowship with one another,
and the blood of Jesus His Son cleanses us from all sin.
1 JOHN 1:6–7

Few things are more enjoyable for a golfer than sitting around the clubhouse or the coffee shop after a round of golf and rehashing the day's round with friends, playing partners, or anyone else who will listen. At the "nineteenth hole," excuses are cast to the wind, all hyperbole is accepted, and the conversation is lively as friends discuss the great shots they made, could have made, or should have made.

As Chi Chi Rodriguez, the great golf philosopher (and not a bad player, either), once observed, "Golf is the only sport that a professional can enjoy playing with his friends. Can Larry Holmes enjoy fighting one of his friends?"[17]

Unquestionably, the camaraderie and fellowship enjoyed by golfers is one of the greatest benefits of the game. If you don't believe it, next time you are seated next to a golfer on a plane or waiting behind a golfer in a line at the grocery store, strike up a marginal conversation about the game. Before you know it, you will be analyzing each other's swings, debating the best new club improvements, and planning a get-together on the links in the near future.

Golfers seem to be members of one large family. They are interested in each other, help each other, and although they compete fiercely against one another, continue to share hopes and dreams for better numbers on the scorecard.

In a real way, the family of God, the Body of Christ, shares a similar sort of fellowship. We enjoy gathering together, we look forward to helping each other, and in truth, we really need each other. God does not want us to be Lone Rangers; He intends for us to function within a body, His Church, the universal Body of Christ. When one person in the family has a problem, we should do whatever we can to solve it; when someone scores a major victory, we all have something to shout about. The apostle Paul put it this way, "If one member suffers, all the members suffer with it; if one member is honored, all the members rejoice with it" (1 Corinthians 12:26).

On the golf course, that may mean that we are quick to offer a word of encouragement to our fellow players: "Great shot!" "Ooh, you were so close on that one." "You are really hitting the ball well." At other times, a word of consolation might be in order: "You were robbed on that one." "I thought sure that putt was going to break, but it didn't."

Our words of praise or encouragement must be genuine —and blessed is the player who knows when to keep his or her mouth shut after a fellow player's lousy shot—but all too often, we allow our competitiveness to overshadow our fellowship.

In the early church, fellowship was a key ingredient to success. The Bible records that first-century Christians "were continually devoting themselves to the apostles' teaching and to fellowship, to the breaking of bread and to prayer" (Acts 2:42).

Notice the four elements that formed the foundations of their lifestyle. First, they were continually learning more about the Lord Jesus through the apostles' teachings about

His life, death, and resurrection.

Second, they were in fellowship. Nowadays, the term fellowship is used much more loosely than in biblical times. The early Christians spent large amounts of time together, often not in formal worship services, but just hanging out, being together. They genuinely cared for one another, doing whatever was necessary to help each other.

Third, they broke bread together. Some scholars say this implies that they had a religious communion service together, and no doubt, the early Christians did have special times in which they remembered the Lord's suffering and death, just as He had commanded (see 1 Corinthians 11:23–34). More likely, though, the passage means that the early Christians frequently ate their meals together.

Gathering around the lunch or dinner table has always been a pleasant opportunity to get to know fellow believers. In our increasingly isolated world, we could greatly enhance our lives simply by getting together with other believers for an occasional meal. It needn't be elaborate, expensive, or fancy. Many Christian men, for example, have discovered the joy of eating breakfast together at a local coffee shop once every few weeks. Christian women who find the time to gather for a soup and sandwich lunch often find spiritual nourishment as well as physical sustenance.

The fourth foundational element of the early Christian community was prayer—not just prayer for the great issues that plague society, but prayer for each other's everyday needs. Their prayers for each other had a sense of practicality. They prayed for real needs, strength for travels, help in business, wisdom in their relationships.

Today, all of us desperately need this sort of fellowship. We must be the kind of friends to whom others can turn when they are in need, and we should be willing to be vulnerable and accountable to fellow believers. We need to have a safe group in which we are able to express our true thoughts and feelings when we are hurting. Something wonderful, something restorative, something positively healing can take place as we experience real, biblical-style fellowship.

PRAYER

Lord, please surround me with people
with whom I can have genuine fellowship.
May I be the kind of Christian friend who
encourages others not only with my words
but through my life.

FURTHER READING
Ephesians 3:14–21

IDOL WORSHIP

Thou shalt have no other gods before me.
EXODUS 20:3 KJV

If someone approached you today and asked, "Are you worshiping an idol?" most likely you would answer, "No way! What kind of person do you think I am?" Yet an idol is not always a piece of wood or stone. Believe it or not, it can be a game.

Golf is a tremendous game. For a minority of players, it is their profession. For those of us who play it recreationally, it is one of the great joys in life. But if we aren't careful, golf can become an idol.

We must make sure that we keep the game in its proper

place on our priority list. And that position should be far below that of God, our spouse, family, friends, and church. God has commanded that we have no other gods before Him, no false gods, no idols that would draw our love and adoration away from Him.

As PGA champion Paul Azinger has said, "Golf is not my god. Golf is a game. Jesus Christ is my God."[18]

PRAYER
Thank You, Lord, for the opportunity to participate
in activities that are restorative,
that challenge and strengthen me physically,
emotionally, intellectually, and spiritually.
Please give me wisdom to discern
when anything in my life threatens to
move from being a gift to a god.

FURTHER READING
Matthew 19:16–30

INTEGRITY COUNTS

And do not be conformed to this world,
but be transformed by the renewing of your mind,
that you may prove what the will of God is,
that which is good and acceptable and perfect.
ROMANS 12:2

Do you cheat on your taxes? Uh-uh. No way. Do you cheat on your spouse? Nope.

Do you cheat in your golf game? Ah. . .well, er. . .it's just a game, isn't it? It doesn't really mean anything.

Interestingly, many companies are finding that the characteristics displayed by employees on the golf course will eventually show up in their work habits. One CEO will not hire a junior executive before playing golf with him or her. His logic: "You can tell a lot about the way a person handles stress, challenges, opportunities to go for the jugular, and how that person handles success or failure. But what I watch for is the person's integrity; you can read volumes about a person's values by the way they handle themselves on the golf course."

If you are willing to fudge on your scorecard (as in lie), you will probably lie in your work. If you move the ball slightly to give yourself an unfair advantage, you will probably shuffle details, circumstances, or figures to take advantage of someone or to make yourself look good at your job. We often joke about liars and cheaters on the golf course, but maybe it's not such a laughing matter.

God expects us to work and play competitively but without compromise.

PRAYER
Lord, may my life be a living testimony
of what Your Word teaches about character,
morality, values, and personal integrity.

FURTHER READING
2 Corinthians 5:14–21

YOU'RE NOT ALONE

And he said,
"I have been very jealous for the LORD,
the God of hosts. . .
And I alone am left;
and they seek my life,
to take it away."
1 KINGS 19:10

When Ben Crenshaw hit his ball into a palm tree at Palm Springs, his caddie shook the tree, hoping to find Ben's ball. More than two dozen balls fell out of the thick leaves. . .but not one belonged to Crenshaw. Obviously other golfers had made the same mistake.

Sometimes we're tempted to get down on ourselves when we do something wrong, when we fail, blow our Christian testimony, or otherwise mess up. No matter how badly we miss the mark, we are not the first person to fail. Nor will we be the last.

If you are prone to depression over your golf game (or anything else, for that matter), take heart. You are not alone. Depression happens to some of the most devout men and women the world has ever seen, people in whom and through whom God has performed miraculous wonders. The prophet Elijah was such a person.

Elijah is well-known for his great faith in God and his miraculous feats done in the name of the Lord. But he could be just as well-known for his fears, frustrations, and deep despair. Elijah is best-known, perhaps, for his spectacular "calling down fire" escapade, in which by faith in God, Elijah defeated 450 prophets of Baal and 400 prophets of the Asherah, all of whom were operating under the direct auspices of sleazy Queen Jezebel, the wife of Ahab, the king of Israel. What an incredible spiritual high that must have been!

But then Ahab reported to Jezebel all that Elijah had done: how he had first embarrassed, and then killed the false prophets. When Jezebel heard this report, she flew into a fury and sent a message to Elijah: "So may the gods do to me and even more, if I do not make your life as the life of one of them by tomorrow about this time" (1 Kings 19:2).

When Elijah heard the words of this woman, "he was afraid and arose and ran for his life" (v. 3). No doubt, Jezebel's threats dashed Elijah's great expectations. After all, he had successfully challenged and defeated the prophets of Baal in the name of the Lord. In only a few days, he had gone from obscurity to national recognition.

Or maybe Elijah experienced a sudden puncture in his spiritual tire and thought, *Oh, no! I just can't take anymore, God. Won't the pressure ever stop? Doesn't life with You ever get any easier? Can't I get a break here?*

We don't know Elijah's exact thoughts, but we can trace his downward spiritual spiral. He tumbles from a magnificent mountaintop experience with God into fear, depression, doubt about God and himself, discouragement, disillusionment, and despair. Elijah even began thinking of self-destruction. He lamented, "I have been very zealous for the LORD, the God of hosts; for the sons of Israel have forsaken Thy covenant, torn down Thine altars and killed Thy prophets with the sword. And I alone am left; and they seek my life, to take it away" (v. 10). Elijah was down and out for the count.

But God was not about to allow Elijah to wallow in the pit for long. God gave him rest, food, and water, and then God gave him a fresh vision of His majesty and power. And Elijah was not only impressed, he was revived. Soon afterward, the Lord gave Elijah a fresh assignment.

Just as Elijah was encouraged by being reminded that there were 7,000 other godly people in Israel, remember: There are many fellow believers walking the links. Be encouraged! You are not alone.

PRAYER
Sometimes I really do feel as though I am
the only believer in my circle of friends,
but let me walk with You, Lord,
in such a way that even if I am the only one,
others will soon believe in You as well.

FURTHER READING
1 Kings 19:1–18

OUR THOUGHTS
MAKE A DIFFERENCE

Finally, brethren, whatever is true,
whatever is honorable, whatever is right,
whatever is pure, whatever is lovely,
whatever is of good repute,
if there is any excellence and
if anything worthy of praise,
let your mind dwell on these things.
PHILIPPIANS 4:8

When Tommy Armour III shot a 4–under par 67 at the 1998 Nissan Open in Valencia, California, he was asked the usual question: "What are you doing differently?" At thirty-eight years of age, Armour had lost his tour card in 1997 but had been permitted to enter the 1998 Nissan tournament on a sponsor's exemption. Suddenly he was atop the leader board. His answer: "I've been coming to the course ready to play good golf."[19]

Attitude does make a difference, doesn't it? Our mind is an amazing computer which will help bring to pass those things that we focus on—whether positively or negatively. And what we focus our thoughts on will make a difference in how we live. Today, choose to think on those things that will improve your performance.

PRAYER
God, whether I am a winner or not
in the eyes of the world,
let me see myself as the
incredibly valuable person
that You say I am.

FURTHER READING
Psalm 139:14–16

IT'S A MENTAL GAME

Have this attitude in yourselves
which was also in Christ Jesus.
PHILIPPIANS 2:5

Anyone who has ever played a round of golf knows that the game is more mental than physical. Yes, swinging a club seventy to ninety (or more) times can be tiring; walking the course rather than riding in a cart will take some energy, too. But the real game is played in the mind.

Here is where our self-image comes into play. Our self-image acts as a comfort zone, that area in which we comfortably see ourselves performing. It is almost impossible to consistently perform on a level higher than we see ourselves. There's truth in the old saying, "Whether you think you can or can't, you're right."

Our self-image acts in a way similar to a thermostat in our home. If the temperature of our house falls below the current setting, the thermostat will kick on the heat. If the temperature rises above the current setting, the thermostat will turn off the heat, or perhaps turn on the air conditioning, in order to bring the temperature back into the comfort zone.

In the same way, our self-image will pull us back into our comfort zone of performance. If we play better than we see ourselves being able to, our self-image will bring us down; if we perform worse than we see ourselves being able to, our self-image can help pull us back up.

That's why it is so important for us to maintain a positive mental attitude by thinking about the things we can do, not on what we can't; expressing what we want to see happen, rather than what we hope to avoid.

In our spiritual lives, our mental attitude is also important. Paul encouraged us in Philippians to have the same attitudes that Christ has. The theme of Charles Sheldon's classic book, *In His Steps,* was "What would Jesus do?" In recent years, the book has once again become popular, spawning a plethora of new merchandise bearing the same question. But when it comes to our attitude, a better question might be,

"What would Jesus think?" Make it a habit to focus on those thoughts that you believe Christ would have.

PRAYER
Father, even more than positive thinking,
I want to have Christlike thoughts.
When I am tempted to allow my mind to wander
into negative or destructive thought patterns,
give me the will to think with the mind of Christ.

FURTHER READING
Romans 12:3; Philippians 2:3; Colossians 1:27

YOU DESERVE A BREAK

Remember the sabbath day, to keep it holy.
Six days you shall labor and do all your work,
but the seventh day is a sabbath
of the LORD your God;
in it you shall not do any work.
EXODUS 20:8–10

Although it may be hard to believe, even our golf game can become wearisome if we make it work. That's why most teachers caution against practicing when tired. Fatigue will lead to frustration, which will lead to failed shots and a loss of confidence. Who needs it?

A better question: Who needs a break one day per week?

We all do. God designed a sabbath, a break in the action, once every seven days. To neglect a weekly day of rest and relaxation will eventually lead to burnout. Remember: Even God rested on the seventh day!

Many Christians fail to take the Sabbath day seriously, and we do so at our own peril. God did not create us to be perpetual motion machines. He has set aside special times for His people to come together, to praise and worship Him, and to rest and be refreshed.

In the Old Testament, Sabbath-breaking was considered a capital crime, punishable by death (Exodus 35:2). In the New Testament, there is no such penalty. But a type of death sentence may still exist for those who neglect to take at least one day per week for rest, reflection, refreshment, and redirection.

We don't need to be legalistic about keeping the Sabbath. In fact, the New Testament does not even say when and how we should keep the Sabbath. This frees believers in many ways. What is relaxing and refreshing for one person may be work for another. A round of golf on Sunday afternoon might be a relaxing activity for some people, but for others it might be sheer frustration and work.

However you choose to observe the Sabbath, it is a reminder of the Lord's reign in your life. Something restorative happens when you are able to set aside one day out of seven and take it as a Sabbath.

PRAYER
Busy, busy, busy; oh, Lord God,
I am so busy that I often allow myself to
crowd You right out of my schedule.
Help me to establish and maintain
special times when I can draw closer to Your heart,
times when You can reorganize my priorities,
helping me to keep my problems and opportunities
in proper perspective.

FURTHER READING
Exodus 20:8–11

KEEP
A LIGHT GRIP

I have been crucified with Christ;
and it is no longer I who live,
but Christ lives in me;
and the life which I now live in the flesh
I live by faith in the Son of God,
who loved me,
and delivered Himself up for me.
GALATIANS 2:20

When it comes to gripping a golf club, most pros and teachers agree: Easy does it. Ben Hogan encouraged golfers to picture holding the club as if holding a tiny, live bird. As surely as squeezing that little bird could result in harm or death to the creature, gripping our golf clubs too tightly could squeeze the life out of our shots.

Similarly, holding too tightly to most anything in life is usually a prescription for trouble. Maybe that's why the apostle Paul learned to live life openhandedly. He said, "I have been crucified with Christ"; his hands (representing his self-will, his own way, his ability to manipulate) were open and the "nail" was in the most sensitive spot. Whatever Christ wanted was what Paul wanted. . .and what we should want, too.

But keeping a light grip is not as easy as it sounds. In golf, there is an incredible temptation to squeeze the club too tightly. Inevitably, this will result in errant shots. Likewise in life, as much as we know the spiritual principle that we should allow Christ to be in charge of our lives, there is always a strong temptation to try to regrip, grasping a little tighter, trying to control things on our own. And just as surely, when we tighten our grip on anything but Jesus, we are closing our fist against God.

Learning to trust Him will be a lifelong adventure, and it is a process in which we find ourselves having to go back for lessons again and again. Over time, though, just as a good golfer learns to hold onto the club with precisely the right amount of pressure, we will learn to discern "God's part" and "our part" in the swing of things.

PRAYER

Lord, teach me to want what You want,
to will what You will,
and to live as You desire for me to live,
with You in control of my life.

FURTHER READING
Romans 8:1–17

PERFECT IS A LONG SHOT

"Therefore you are to be perfect,
as your heavenly Father is perfect."
MATTHEW 5:48

Dead, solid, perfect" is a phrase used by skilled golfers to describe a shot that is exceptionally well-placed, as in: "I hit that one pin-high, dead, solid, perfect." But if it were really the perfect shot, it would have gone into the hole, right?

Obviously, "perfect" is a relative term on the golf course. You hit a beautiful drive right out the center of the fairway, get a great roll, and then your ball slows to a stop. As you walk up to your ball, you realize that you are in an ideal spot to hit the green in regulation. "Perfect shot!" your playing partner calls from the rough where his ball is still buried.

"Thanks," you reply a bit hesitantly.

It was a perfect shot, yet deep inside you feel that if you would have executed just a little bit better, perhaps had you brought your hips around further or kept the club more steady, you might have hit an even better shot! "Perfect," but not quite good enough.

Why does that sense of imperfection persist, even when we perform at peak levels? Because perfect is a long shot.

No wonder Jesus' followers were shocked when, in the middle of His Sermon on the Mount (one of the most nitty-gritty, down-to-earth, practical passages in Scripture), Jesus said, "Therefore you are to be perfect, as your heavenly Father is perfect."

Jesus' listeners must have reeled. "Perfect? Who can possibly live a perfect life? Especially after all the standards You have just given us: Don't lust in your heart; don't get so angry that you call your brother a fool; love your enemies, and all the rest! You must be kidding, Jesus. No one can be perfect against those kinds of pars."

But the word perfect as it is used here does not necessarily mean perfect performance; it means "mature, complete." Nevertheless, many Christians say, "Perfection is an admirable goal, something at which to aim, but it is totally unattainable in this life." They see the ideals of the Christian life as something they should shoot for, but they know and God knows that they are never going to really live it "dead, solid, perfect." We might as well not even try. As a result, many sincere believers have condemned themselves to subpar Christian living, resigning themselves to failure and frustration, never really expecting to live by biblical standards because, after all, no matter what effort they put forth, it is impossible to please God anyhow.

And in a way, they are absolutely right.

In our own power, with our own physical, intellectual, and spiritual strength, we will never live up to God's standards of perfection. But never underestimate the power of the Holy Spirit to shape us into the people God has called us to be. Scripture says, " 'Not by might nor by power, but by My Spirit,' says the LORD of hosts" (Zechariah 4:6). With God's power working in us, it is possible to be perfect in His sight. As we surrender our will to Him on a daily (momentary!) basis, His Spirit takes over and provides the "on-board guidance system" we need to live in a way that pleases God and impacts society in His name.

Under our own strength, no matter how well we perform, we will always have the sense that our life is disoriented, confused, and not accomplishing anything of real significance. "My life is coming apart. The wheels are coming off," some people say. They are disintegrated. But when we allow Jesus to be in control, He integrates everything in our lives, pulling it all back together, putting everything in its proper perspective, and giving us a positive purpose to live. Because we are relying on His perfection rather than on our own, we know we are accepted by Him, and we exude a confidence that is impossible to achieve through any other means. Now that is "dead, solid, perfect."

PRAYER
God, in my spiritual life just as in golf,
it seems that my best is not good enough.
I acknowledge that in my daily life,
in my own righteousness or goodness,
I would not qualify to be in Your kingdom.
But I thank You, Lord,
that I do not rely on my own performance
or personal perfection.
Instead I rely on Your Word,
Your blood which purchased my redemption,
and Your power to help me live correctly.

FURTHER READING
Matthew 5; Revelation 21:1– 22:17

WHEN YOU DON'T GET WHAT YOU WANT

"How is it that your spirit is so sullen?"
1 KINGS 21:5

King Hasson of Morocco enjoyed the game of golf, but he was having a bit of trouble with his sand shots, playing out of the bunkers on the nine-hole palace course. Instead of working on his deficiency, the king ordered that the bunkers should be filled with sod.[20]

Nearly three thousand years earlier, another king in that part of the world, Ahab, looked at his neighbor's vineyard and wanted it. When the owner wouldn't sell, Ahab's wife, Queen

Jezebel, had the owner killed, and then Ahab confiscated the vineyard.

Selfishness is a horribly destructive trait. "I want what I want when I want it" is the essence of sin. We may, indeed, get what we want, but if we win by deceit, fraud, cheating, lowering our standards, or in any other improper manner, our success will bring us sadness rather than joy.

Instead of constantly complaining about what we don't have, what we cannot do, where we cannot go, let's begin to develop a habit of thanking God for what we do have, what we can do, where we are free to go. We will be amazed by how our lives begin to change when we allow the Lord to reconstruct our wish lists.

PRAYER
Lord, there are many things in this world
that look so appealing to me.
Help me to be content with what I have,
while constantly striving to adopt Your point of view
concerning those things that really matter.

FURTHER READING
1 Thessalonians 5:18; Psalm136

KEEP AT IT

And let us not lose heart in doing good,
for in due time we shall reap if we do not grow weary.
GALATIANS 6:9

The old saying, "Practice makes perfect" may or may not be true, but most things that are worth doing well take practice, and the time allotted to practice usually far exceeds that of the actual performance. In the 1938 movie *Carefree,* Fred Astaire hit a row of golf balls while tap-dancing. To get the scene on film took ten days of rehearsal and two days of filming, during which Astaire hit nearly a thousand practice shots. When the movie was released, the scene lasted three minutes.

Similarly we need diligence if we hope to make progress in our spiritual lives. The saying, "No pain, no gain," has a lot of truth to it. When the apostle Paul was encouraging the early Christians at Philippi, he wrote: "Work out your salvation with fear and trembling; for it is God who is at work in you, both to will and to work for His good pleasure. Do all things without grumbling or disputing; that you may prove yourselves to be blameless and innocent, children of God above reproach in the midst of a crooked and perverse generation, among whom you appear as lights in the world" (Philippians 2:12–15).

Notice that Paul implied that the Christian life is not one of ease; it takes work. Certainly God is at work in us, and it is His power on which we must depend, but there are some things He requires us to do in this refining process. We must work on our spiritual life, while He works on us. As we keep learning, applying our spiritual disciplines, and expanding our horizons, God will show us more and more of His plan for our lives.

It won't be easy, but it will be worth it in the end. Perseverance will never be popular, but it is still the price tag for perfection.

PRAYER
Father, help me not to always choose the easy way
but rather the way that pleases You the most.

FURTHER READING
Luke 11:1–13

THE PROS AND CONS
OF ANGER

Be angry, and yet do not sin;
do not let the sun go down on your anger,
and do not give the devil an opportunity.
EPHESIANS 4:26–27

Most pro golfers know that one of the surest ways to wreck opponents' concentration is to get them mad. A few pros are able to make anger work for them as a motivator, but most players simply continue a downhill slide if they cannot overcome their anger. Don't get mad while playing. It is a sure way to lose.

Ironically, the Bible says it is possible to get angry and

yet not sin. When we get angry at sin, rather than some imposition on our rights, we are angry for the right reason. For example, when we get angry at injustices in our society, or at the senseless deaths of drive-by shootings, or at rape and plunder by totalitarian despots, we are exercising a proper anger. No matter what the horror, however, we must direct our anger at the sin rather than at the person who commits the sin. Anger in these situations can motivate us to righteous responses.

But when we try to defend our egos, pride, prestige, or position, or when we lash out at another person in anger, we have sinned. If we can't express something in love, we shouldn't say it.

In any case, don't carry anger with you. Get it out of your system by dealing with it today. You may have to stay up late to get the problem solved, but you will sleep much better, and your outlook tomorrow will be transformed.

PRAYER
Father, please help me to be more concerned
about doing what is right than about
constantly defending my own rights.

FURTHER READING
Exodus 32

KEEP UP THE ENERGY

Rejoice always; pray without ceasing;
in everything give thanks;
for this is God's will for you in Christ Jesus.
1 THESSALONIANS 5:16–18

You pull your cart up to the first tee, smack a long drive out the fairway, and head off for a rousing round of golf. But about halfway through the front nine, your cart begins to die. It is barely chugging up the hills and coasting down the grades. *What's wrong with this thing?* you wonder. After nine holes of frustration, you are tired of fooling with the sputtering vehicle, so you pull the cart in to the clubhouse and demand a new cart before traversing the back nine.

The fellow at the cart barn pulls up the seat and takes a look. "I'm really sorry," he says. "Looks like somebody forgot to charge up the battery last night. Ordinarily, we plug in the carts overnight and allow them to charge so they are ready for a busy day on the course first thing in the morning."

We, too, need our spiritual batteries charged each day. It's tough to last for very long when we try to survive on yesterday's spiritual charge. We find ourselves succumbing to temptations that we would ordinarily reject, tolerating conduct and attitudes that under normal circumstances we would view as repugnant. In short, our defenses are down, and the enemy usually takes advantage of any opportunity to beat us.

That's why it is important to establish some spiritual disciplines that will work for us on a daily basis. Like our golf game, consistency is what counts, not quantity. Try reading a page or two from your Bible every morning before you get into the flow of your day. While devotional books are a helpful supplement, they are no substitute for the Word of God in your life.

Similarly, take a few minutes to acknowledge your need of the Lord's help. Surrender control of your life to Him afresh each morning, asking God to direct your paths and help you to make wise choices. Pray that God will help you to use your time in the best manner possible to accomplish those things that are important to Him. As you establish some basic spiritual disciplines, you will be surprised at your energy level, your effectiveness, and your improved attitude.

Another way to charge your spiritual battery is to make church attendance a priority in your life. Amazingly, many Christians tend to drain their spiritual batteries because they are not plugged in to a good, Bible-believing church. Don't ignore the power that comes from being connected with other believers on a regular basis. You will come away recharged, refreshed, and ready to meet and overcome the hazards and obstacles you are sure to encounter on life's course.

PRAYER
Show me those things, Father,
that are expedient, those things that are necessary,
and those things that are absolutely essential
for my spiritual health.
Then give me the courage to choose those
which are most beneficial to
Your kingdom and to me.

FURTHER READING
Hebrews 10:19–25

LITTLE BIG MAN

And he was trying to see who Jesus was,
and he was unable because of the crowd,
for he was small in stature.
LUKE 19:3

During the 1995 U.S. Open, the small-of-stature Corey Pavin was paired with Vijay Singh and Davis Love III for the first two rounds. Both Singh and Love hit the ball a mile, while Pavin hits it short and straight. Nevertheless, Pavin won the Open and took home a check for $350,000. He later said, "I am not the biggest or strongest guy, but that certainly is not a prerequisite to win a U.S. Open."[21]

Nor is physical stature a factor in our relationship with

God. In the Bible, although Zaccheus was a little fellow, he had a big desire to see Jesus. He climbed a tree to get a better look as Jesus was passing by. When Jesus saw him, the Lord called Zaccheus by name, and invited Himself for a visit at the little man's home—an honor that only a few people in history are known to have had.

Few people nowadays claim to have seen Jesus personally. But we can be certain of Jesus' promise that those who believe by faith will be blessed.

After the resurrection, Thomas, one of Jesus' disciples, remained skeptical. Others had seen Jesus alive from the dead; they had walked with Him, talked with Him, eaten with Him, and had observed Him with their own eyes and ears. But Thomas had not been with them during those times. He declared, "Unless I shall see in His hands the imprint of the nails, and put my finger into the place of the nails, and put my hand into His side, I will not believe" (John 20:25).

About a week later, Thomas was with the other disciples, and Jesus appeared. Ever gracious, Jesus offered Thomas the opportunity to touch His hands, to put his hand into His side, to examine for himself whether Jesus was alive again.

"Be not unbelieving, but believing," Jesus told Thomas (v. 27).

When Thomas saw for himself that Jesus was alive, he

answered, "My Lord and my God!" (v. 28). Apparently, being in the presence of Jesus was all the proof Thomas needed to believe. Scripture does not mention Thomas going ahead and touching Jesus.

Then Jesus said to Thomas, "Because you have seen Me, have you believed? Blessed are they who did not see, and yet believed" (v. 29).

That includes us! Although we have not seen Jesus with our physical eyes, we have believed, and we have been blessed through our faith in Christ.

Skeptics have always been with us and always will be. Upon the death of the renowned scientist Carl Sagan, one of his relatives was asked if Sagan believed in God. "Carl never wanted to believe," came the response; "Carl wanted to know."[22] Unfortunately, knowledge about Jesus will never be sufficient. We must believe in Him, trust Him with our lives.

When your desire is to see Jesus, nothing else matters.

PRAYER
Give me spiritual eyes to see, O Lord.
And please give me faith to believe even when I cannot see.

FURTHER READING
John 20

RUNNER-UP

One of the two who. . .followed Him, was Andrew,
Simon Peter's brother. He found first his own brother Simon,
and said to him, "We have found the Messiah"
(which translated means Christ).
JOHN 1:40–41

Few people have finished second in more PGA Tour events than Greg Norman. Although he has won numerous tournaments and an enormous amount of money, Norman's runner-up status often gets more attention than his trophies. He is often criticized for his tendency to come in second. Greg Norman sees it differently. He says, "I've put myself in position with a chance to win more times than anybody else."[23]

We don't usually remember the guy who comes in second. There is an old saying that the most difficult instrument to play in an orchestra is second violin. Sometimes the person behind the scenes is the one who makes it possible for the person out front to succeed. Most of us remember Peter, the great disciple of Jesus and leader of the early church. But who was Andrew? What did he ever do worth remembering? Nothing much. He just introduced his brother to Jesus. But think what an impact that one action had on the course of history.

You may not be the best player on the course, but watch for opportunities to introduce others to Jesus, and you can be certain they will come. Remember, if you truly know Christ, you have the answer to the questions the world is asking; you possess the priceless treasure for which so many people are still searching. You needn't be bashful or self-conscious about your faith. You have much to share.

PRAYER
Lord, sometimes I'm intimidated by others who are older, stronger, or more talented than I am. Help me to be confident in the truth, bold in sharing my faith in You, and certain that Your Word will never return void.

FURTHER READING
John 4:1–42

SEESAW DAYS!

In the day of prosperity be happy,
But in the day of adversity consider—
God has made the one as well as the other.
ECCLESIASTES 7:14

Club pro Blair Gibson was playing a practice round before the 1996 Honda Classic when he decided to go for the pin in two on the long, par-five eighteenth green. To do so, Gibson's shot had to clear a lake in which one of the sponsor's new vehicles was perched on an "island." Gibson flubbed his shot and the ball streaked toward the lake, a certain lost ball and a penalty stroke to boot. Instead of hitting the water, however, Gibson's ball slammed off the top of the Honda and bounced to within twelve feet of the cup. Gibson made his putt for eagle.

Some days are like that. Every stroke you make seems to be the right one; you can do nothing wrong. Then at other times, you can't seem to find the hole. You feel as though you are on a seesaw, up one moment, down the next.

It's easy to feel God's presence on those days when everything is going right. But guard against getting discouraged when you have bad days. God is still with you, and your future with Him is bright.

PRAYER
In good times or in bad,
when I am surrounded by people
or when it seems that I am all alone,
let me be reminded, O Lord,
that You are right there with me,
that I am never really alone,
and that You will see me through.

FURTHER READING
Matthew 28:16–20; Hebrews 4:12–16

SOME GIMMES
AREN'T SO GOOD

And he said,
"A certain man had two sons;
and the younger of them said to his father,
'Father, give me the share of the estate that falls to me.'
And he divided his wealth between them."
Luke 15:11

That's a gimme, isn't it?" is heard time and again on the golf course as another close-but-no-banana putt stops short of the cup. The "gimme," the time-honored tradition of giving close putts to competitors without forcing them to grind out that last shot has come to be expected.

In Luke 15, the prodigal son had that gimme attitude when he had the audacity to ask his father for his inheritance before the father was even sick, let alone dead and gone. The prodigal's gimme attitude, however, was soon matched by his "friends," who sucked him dry of Dad's money and then dumped him. The prodigal soon learned that the gimme was the fastest way to the pigpen.

Fortunately, when he came to his senses, he said, "I will get up and go to my father, and will say to him, 'Father, I have sinned' " (v. 18). Now that's a good place to start when we want a cure for a "gimme attitude."

PRAYER
Father, please help me to
develop a giving attitude,
rather than a give me attitude.

FURTHER READING
Luke 6:38; 15:11–32

THE GREAT EQUALIZER

"Otherwise, you may say in your heart,
'My power and the strength of my hand
made me this wealth.'
But you shall remember the LORD your God,
for it is He who is giving you
power to make wealth,
that He may confirm His covenant which
He swore to your fathers,
as it is this day."
DEUTERONOMY 8:17–18

After qualifying for the 1993 Buick Open, club pro Craig
Thomas turned around and shot a 92 in the first round of the

tournament. The golf course is truly the great equalizer: One day we may bring it to its knees, and the next day we may be on our knees, begging for mercy. It's easy to get cocky when we are doing well, but remember, another day is coming.

Moses gave the Israelites a similar warning when they were about to cross into the Promised Land. Essentially Moses told them, "When you start doing well, remember it is not just your power and ability that has caused you to be successful. It is God's power at work in you, and He is doing it so He can work out His plan in your life and in the lives of others."

Becoming arrogant or complacent in our success is just as dangerous as becoming depressed or frustrated in our failure. Many people who have survived tough times or difficult days succumb to the temptations brought about by their success.

As God's people were about to enter the Promised Land, the Lord had great plans for them, plans for good, not for evil. But He knew that His children would encounter many temptations in Canaan (a land of abundance) that they had not previously experienced in the arid wilderness through which they had been tramping for years. That's why Moses gave God's people such a stern warning: "Beware lest you forget the LORD your God by not keeping His commandments" (Deuteronomy 8:11).

We are most vulnerable, most susceptible to Satan's stratagems, when we think we can stand on our own. Always remember the Lord is the One who delivered you, and He is the One—the only One—who can keep you in the day of trouble.

PRAYER
Father, let my confidence be in You,
in Your strength rather than my own.
I am very much aware of Your blessings in my life,
and I appreciate every one.
But may I never become so foolish as to think
that the blessings You have bestowed on me
have been earned on my own or deserved
because of my talent or gifts.
Without You, I could do nothing.

FURTHER READING
Deuteronomy 8; Luke 12:15–34

THE DUES HAVE BEEN PAID

He made Him who knew no sin
to be sin on our behalf,
that we might become the
righteousness of God in Him.
2 CORINTHIANS 5:21

No matter how talented, charming, or experienced a professional golfer may be, he cannot play in any PGA Tour event until he has paid the $100 annual membership fee. Similarly, at many private golf courses, people are not allowed on the course unless they are a member of the club or a guest. In some elite clubs, even money is irrelevant; membership is by vote only.

Thankfully, when it comes to being allowed in "God's club," no vote can keep us out and no amount of money is necessary to get in. The price has been paid in blood, the blood of Jesus Christ. The Lord Jesus paid our dues for us, once and for all; admission is now free to anyone who wants to enter.

Though it may seem incomprehensible to our finite minds, when Jesus died on the cross, He took upon Himself the disease of our sin; He who was absolutely pure took on our awful impurity. The price was high: It cost Him His life, but as a result, we are able to live. That's what the apostle Paul was talking about when he wrote, "He made Him who knew no sin to be sin on our behalf, that we might become the righteousness of God in Him" (2 Corinthians 5:21).

The good news of the gospel is this: Although God hates sin and will judge it accordingly, God's wrath over sin does not have to be poured out on us, because the blood of Jesus enables us to have a totally new relationship with Him. We are reconciled to God. His attitude toward us is one of love—amazing, unconditional love!

Our attitude toward Him ought to be the same. When we accept His love—by acknowledging that Jesus paid the penalty for our sin with His blood, repenting of our sins, and seeking His forgiveness—we can be free from sin's deadly domination of our lives. Paul said, "Having now been justified by His blood, we shall be saved from the wrath of God through Him" (Romans 5:9).

The great hymn writer, Charles Wesley, put it this way in his classic:

AND CAN IT BE

And can it be that I should gain.
An int'rest in the Savior's blood?
Died He for me, who caused His pain?
For me, who Him to death pursued?
Amazing love! how can it be
That thou, my God, shouldst die for me?
Amazing love! how can it be
That thou, my God, shouldst die for me?

The blood of Jesus paid the way for us to enter the kingdom of God. The dues have been paid. Go play and enjoy!

PRAYER

Lord, may I be ever conscious of the tremendous price
You paid for my salvation. Please don't ever allow me
to take Your love and grace for granted, but may they
motivate me to love You with all my heart.

FURTHER READING
1 Peter 1:17–25

NOTES

1. Ward Clayton, "A Photographer's Scrapbook," *The Augusta Chronicles* (March 1995), 4.

2. Barry Wilner, *Golf Stories of Today* (Philadelphia, PA: Chelsea House Publishers, 1998), 8, 10.

3. John Feinstein, "Dangers of a Little Knowledge," *Golf* (November 1997): 17.

4. Frank S. Mead, ed., *The Encyclopedia of Religious Quotations* (Old Tappan, NJ: Fleming H. Revell, 1965), 34.

5. James R. Bolley, *The Golfer's Tee Time Devotional* (Tulsa, OK: Honor Books, 1997), 99.

6. Thomas Boswell, *Strokes of Genius* (New York, NY: Doubleday, 1987), 171.

7. Brian Swarbrick, *The Duffer's Guide to Bogey Golf* (Englewood Cliffs, NY: Prentice Hall, 1973), 12, 24.

8. Helen Roseveare, *Living Holiness* (Minneapolis: Bethany House, 1986), 43.

9. Barb Thomas, "It's Not My Money," *The Links Letter* (May/June 1995): vol. 15, no. 3: 3.

10. Rob Tipton, "The Latest Links," *The Links Letter* (November/December 1995): vol. 15, no. 6: 5.

11. Personal author interview.

12. Paul Azinger with Ken Abraham, *Zinger* (New York: Harper Paperbacks, 1995 edition), 195–96.

13. "Material Girl," *People* (April 7, 1986), 52.

14. Adapted from Tom Lehman, *I Felt Like a Failure* (Annondale, VA: Links Players, 1996), 1–2.

15. Thomas Boswell, *Stroke of Genius* (New York: Doubleday, 1987), 156.

16. Henry Beard, *Mulligan's Laws* (New York: Doubleday, 1993), 41.

17. James R. Bolley, *The Golfer's Tee Time Devotional* (Tulsa, OK: Honor Books, 1997), 194.

18. Interview at PGA Press Booth, author interview. February, 1995.

19. Taken from *Golf: Great Thoughts on the Game* (Philadelphia, PA: Running Press, 1995), 24.

20. Floyd Conner, *Great Moments & Dubious Achievements in Golf History* (San Francisco, CA: Chronicle Books, 1992), 18.

21. Interview at PGA Press Booth, author interview. June, 1995.

22. "Unbeliever's Quest," *Newsweek* (March 31, 1997), 41.

23. Rick Reilly, "Master Strokes," *Sports Illustrated* (May 1996), 38.

Ken Abraham is an award-winning author, editor, and compiler of nearly three dozen books, including *Zinger*, a collaboration with professional golfer Paul Azinger. Ken is an avid bogey golfer with dreams of one day breaking ninety. Fortunately, his writing, is "dead, solid, perfect"—right down the middle of the fairway.

Two of Ken's other collaborative efforts include *The Gamer* with 11-time major league baseball All Star Gary Carter, and *Bringing out the Winner in Your Child* with John Croyle. He thoroughly enjoys giving amateur golf lessons to his daughters, Ashleigh and Alyssa, who love to drive the golf cart—or, as they refer to it, their "Barbie car."